Post-Roman and Medieval Drying Kilns

About Access Archaeology

Access Archaeology offers a different publishing model for specialist academic material that might traditionally prove commercially unviable, perhaps due to its sheer extent or volume of colour content, or simply due to its relatively niche field of interest. This could apply, for example, to a PhD dissertation or a catalogue of archaeological data.

All *Access Archaeology* publications are available as a free-to-download pdf eBook and in print format. The free pdf download model supports dissemination in areas of the world where budgets are more severely limited, and also allows individual academics from all over the world the opportunity to access the material privately, rather than relying solely on their university or public library. Print copies, nevertheless, remain available to individuals and institutions who need or prefer them.

The material is refereed and/or peer reviewed. Copy-editing takes place prior to submission of the work for publication and is the responsibility of the author. Academics who are able to supply print-ready material are not charged any fee to publish (including making the material available as a free-to-download pdf). In some instances the material is type-set in-house and in these cases a small charge is passed on for layout work.

Our principal effort goes into promoting the material, both the free-to-download pdf and print edition, where *Access Archaeology* books get the same level of attention as all of our publications which are marketed through e-alerts, print catalogues, displays at academic conferences, and are supported by professional distribution worldwide.

The free pdf download allows for greater dissemination of academic work than traditional print models could ever hope to support. It is common for a free-to-download pdf to be downloaded hundreds or sometimes thousands of times when it first appears on our website. Print sales of such specialist material would take years to match this figure, if indeed they ever would.

This model may well evolve over time, but its ambition will always remain to publish archaeological material that would prove commercially unviable in traditional publishing models, without passing the expense on to the academic (author or reader).

Post-Roman and Medieval Drying Kilns

Foundations of Archaeological Research

Robert Rickett

Edited and with an introduction by Mark McKerracher

Access Archaeology

ARCHAEOPRESS PUBLISHING LTD
Summertown Pavilion
18-24 Middle Way
Summertown
Oxford OX2 7LG
www.archaeopress.com

ISBN 978-1-80327-070-8
ISBN 978-1-80327-071-5 (e-Pdf)

Cover: Replica medieval drying kiln at Ferrycarrig National Heritage Park, Ireland © Colin Morrison, RTÉ Television. Reproduced by kind permission of Colm Crowley, RTÉ Television. First published in *Secrets of the Irish Landscape* (Cork University Press, 2003), edited by Mathew Jebb and Colm Crowley.

This book is available direct from Archaeopress or from our website www.archaeopress.com

I would like to dedicate this study to Dr Mark McKerracher, whose foresight and hard work have made it available for others to use in the future. Thank you.

Robert Rickett

Contents

List of figures

List of tables

Acknowledgements

I should like to thank Dr Michael G. Jarrett for supervising this thesis and advising me on several points, and also for letting me see the site records of the Roman drying kilns at Whitton. Above all I would like to thank all those people, mentioned in the text, who either sent me unpublished information, or let me see the site records of drying kilns; my greatest debt is to Miss Christine M. Mahany, who let me see the site records of several kiln excavations, and allowed me to include much unpublished information. My thanks must also go to Mr Stephen A. Moorhouse for advice and help on several points; to Mr Laurence Tebbutt for lending me his notes on the corn drying kiln which, until recently, stood beside the King's Mill in Stamford; to Mr Terry C. Pearce, who helped me to obtain information on the Glen Parva kiln; and to all those people who kindly sent me information on Roman and post-medieval drying kilns, which, owing to lack of space, were not included in this thesis. Finally, my thanks must also go to Miss Stephanie B. Hilton, for typing this thesis, and for helping me with several points.

Robert Rickett

January 1975

University College, Cardiff

I am very grateful to Dr Mark McKerracher for reading my dissertation and offering to digitise it for publication, as he considers it still useful as a basis for further work by others. Mark's informative introduction places my work into context with what has been achieved since it was written and the current state of knowledge and research. He has done an incredible job, working from a faded copy, devising a simpler reference system which makes it easier to use, giving grid references to each site and producing new distribution maps. He has updated references to sites that are now published. As a result, it is a much better piece of work than the original. Thank you.

I would also like to thank Mr Mick Monk and Dr Rhiannon Comeau for supporting the publication of my dissertation.

Robert Rickett

June 2021

North Elmham, Norfolk

My thanks to Mr Robert Rickett for sharing his dissertation with me, for permitting and supporting its publication, and of course for executing such an important piece of work in the first place – its enduring value, some 45 years on, is testament to the quality of Robert's research. I would also like to thank Mr Mick Monk and Dr Rhiannon Comeau for sharing with me their seminal works on drying kilns, for supporting the publication of this book, and for reading a draft version and providing valuable insights and recommendations. I am grateful to Iliffe Publishing, Current Publishing and the Society of Medieval Archaeology for permission to reproduce images originally published in the *Rutland & Stamford Mercury*, *Current Archaeology* and *Medieval Archaeology* respectively; to Sue Greaney of English Heritage for the photograph of Tintagel; to Samuel Clarke of Historic England for permission to publish material pertaining to the unpublished Grafton Regis excavations; and to Prof. Martin Biddle and the Winchester Excavations Committee for permission to reproduce the photograph of the Winchester kiln.

The maps in this book have been produced using QGIS software (http://www.qgis.org, viewed 29 June 2021); Great Britain and islands boundary data from Ordnance Survey Open Data © Crown copyright and database right 2017, under the Open Government licence; Isle of Man boundary data from Hijmans *et al.* 2015 under the Attribution 3.0 Unported licence (https://creativecommons.org/licenses/by/3.0, viewed 29 June 2021); and island of Ireland boundary data from *Irish Townlands* (https://www.townlands.ie, viewed 29 June 2021) using OpenStreetMap data © OpenStreetMap contributors, under the Open Data Commons Open Database licence (http://opendatacommons.org/licenses/odbl, viewed 29 June 2021).

Mark McKerracher

June 2021

University of Oxford

Introduction

Mark McKerracher (2021)

When I began researching the corn-drying kilns of early medieval England in 2010, I found a subject which (to say the least) had not been over-studied. There was no lack of material, but rather a lack of synthesis. Numerous Anglo-Saxon corn-drying or malting kilns had been excavated by then, and although they were not as familiar and ubiquitous as their Romano-British counterparts, archaeologists had begun to divine their economic significance (e.g. Hamerow 2012: 151–155). Yet there appeared to be no publications dedicated specifically to the archaeology of drying ovens/kilns in Anglo-Saxon and medieval England. By contrast, the archaeology of drying kilns in early medieval Ireland was evidently an active and well-published field of research, advanced in particular by the work of Mick Monk of University College Cork.

Whilst exploring the work of Monk and his colleagues, I realised that a foundational study in the archaeology of drying kilns, in both early medieval Britain and Ireland, was an undergraduate dissertation submitted for a Bachelor's degree at University College Cardiff (now Cardiff University) in 1975. More than four decades later, Robert Rickett's *Post-Roman and Medieval Drying Kilns* remains a seminal work on the subject. Its scope is remarkably ambitious, taking in diverse drying kilns from across England, Scotland, Wales, the island of Ireland and the Isle of Man, and drawing upon both historical and archaeological evidence. Unfortunately, as I soon discovered, this work had never been published. In 2012, I was able to study the original dissertation in Cardiff University library for a single afternoon, as part of my doctoral research (McKerracher 2014a). Returning to the topic in 2019, however, I learned that the library no longer held undergraduate dissertations in its collection, and I was unable to locate the copy which I had seen in 2012. At the time of writing, its ultimate fate remains unknown to me.

I was therefore relieved and grateful to find that Mr Rickett was happy to lend me his personal copy, and to grant permission for its publication. Hence this book presents, some 45 years after its completion, a pioneering study of post-Roman and medieval drying kilns, explicitly intended to be 'a basis for future studies' (see page 4). I have digitised and edited the text and figures to enhance their utility and clarity, and I have added notes to the Gazetteer (see page 39) highlighting where, to the best of my knowledge, excavations discussed by Rickett have been published since 1975. Otherwise, the original dissertation's arguments, observations and evidential base remain intact in this book. No attempt has been made to update the content with post-1975 discoveries and ideas, as this would have obscured the real context and purpose of this book as a foundation or departure point for the topic based upon the evidence available around the advent of modern archaeology.

Nevertheless, a lot of relevant work has been undertaken since 1975. Within four years of Rickett's remark that 'a new assessment of the Roman drying kilns is needed' (see page 4), such an assessment duly appeared in Morris's *Agricultural Buildings in Roman Britain* (Morris 1979: 5–22). Alongside a detailed account of Romano-British corn-dryers, Morris assembled a large and important corpus of excavated examples and devised a corn-dryer typology. Though still useful, this corpus has largely been superseded by that of the *Rural Settlement of Roman Britain* project, which identified corn-dryers at 358

1

excavated rural settlements; their forms, construction, functions and distribution are covered in Lodwick's exemplary discussion (in Allen *et al.* 2017: 55–62).

Besides Morris' seminal survey, 1979 also saw the publication of an experiment at Butser Ancient Farm, where a replica of the Romano-British 'corn-dryer' excavated at Foxholes Farm (Hertfordshire) was found to be inefficient at drying corn but effective for malting (Reynolds and Langley 1979). The results only hold true, of course, for that particular reconstruction with – significantly – an impermeable drying floor. By contrast, Kelleher's experiments in Ireland achieved different results by using replica 'keyhole-shaped' structures with permeable drying floors (Monk and Kelleher 2005). Reynolds and Langley anticipated such a difference, and draw a distinction between the 'corn-drying kilns in the Northern Isles' and 'the so-called Romano-British corn-driers' (Reynolds and Langley 1979: 39) – though there is no reason to assume that all Romano-British corn-dryers were constructed like the Butser replica. Indeed, the excavator of the original Foxholes Farm kiln, Clive Partridge, was not entirely convinced that the drying floor had been impermeable (Mick Monk, pers. comm.).

A terminological distinction echoing Reynolds and Langley's functional distinction persists in much of the archaeological literature. Roman examples are typically called 'corn-drying ovens', 'corn-driers' or 'corndryers' (e.g. Lodwick in Allen *et al.* 2017), whereas Scottish and Irish examples are generally 'corn-drying *kilns*' (e.g. Dixon 2011; Monk and Power 2012). For post-Roman examples in Wales and England, 'grain dryer/drier', 'drying oven' and (particularly in Wales) 'drying kiln' are all common and often interchangeable (e.g. Britnell 1984; Heaton 1993; McKerracher 2014b). I am not aware that drying kiln terminology has been discussed at length in any publication, but two basic points may be noted here. The first (pedantic) point is that 'dryer', a noun, is arguably preferable to 'drier', usually an adjective. The second (semantic) point is that Rickett draws a useful distinction between kilns and ovens – the former intended for drying, the latter for baking (e.g. below, page 19) – and uses the generic term 'drying kiln' to allow for the variety of commodities that could be dried in the very same structures (see below, pages 20-22; Rickett's recognition that drying kilns were often likely multi-purpose remains an important contribution). An analogous distinction between ovens and kilns appears in twelfth- and thirteenth-century Welsh legal texts, which differentiate between an oven or furnace – *ffwrn* – and a dryer or kiln – *odyn* – a term still current in the 19th century (Rhiannon Comeau pers. comm.; Butler 1987: 53–54; Comeau and Burrow 2021).

While Morris' 1979 survey focused on Romano-British 'corn-dryers', research on post-Roman 'drying kilns' was carried on by Monk (1981), building upon his analysis of archaeobotanical remains from kilns excavated at Poundbury (Dorset), his experience as a field archaeologist, and his involvement in projects such as Butser Ancient Farm. He pioneered an archaeobotanical approach to the interpretation of kiln functions, which foreshadowed van der Veen's influential 1989 paper on the charred plant remains found in Roman corn-dryers (van der Veen 1989). Whilst working in Cardiff on the Poundbury plant remains, Monk read Rickett's unpublished work, which had been written before environmental sampling for plant remains had become routine excavation practice. Following his appointment as lecturer at University College Cork in 1978, the focus of Monk's work shifted from England to the drying kilns of Ireland, and this is perhaps why Rickett's influence has been stronger in Irish archaeology than in British research (Monk and Kelleher 2005: 78). The work of Monk and his colleagues has tracked the ever-growing corpus of Irish drying kilns, exploring chronological and distributional patterns and the wider significance of these increasingly ubiquitous discoveries (e.g. Monk and Power 2012; 2014). In addition, the monumental *Early Medieval Archaeology Project* has comprehensively surveyed drying kiln evidence in the wider context of early medieval Irish agriculture (O'Sullivan *et al.* 2014). To my knowledge, no similarly comprehensive surveys of early medieval archaeology have been undertaken for Scotland, Wales, England, or the Isle of Man (though for some general coverage of the latter, see Davey 2014; McDonald 2019).

The study of Scottish drying kilns has benefited from the publication of Fenton's ethnographic work (Fenton 1978), and more recently from a survey by Dixon focusing on kilns of the 12th to mid-18th centuries (Dixon 2011). The first comprehensive survey of Welsh drying kilns has recently been completed by Comeau and Burrow: a tour de force of synthesis and interpretation, encompassing late prehistoric, Roman, post-Roman and medieval instances up to the 16th century (Comeau and Burrow 2021). Their gazetteer includes a further evolution of the kiln typology developed by Monk, which in turn represented an evolution of Rickett's scheme (Monk and Kelleher 2005; this volume, page 39). An important development has been the recognition that, whereas Rickett's typology is dominated by stone-built kilns, many kilns are now known with little or no stone lining (see, for example, the 'pear-shaped' dryers in Comeau and Burrow 2021) – likely a consequence, in part, of improved identification of non-stone structures in modern archaeology.

For England, Rickett noted that 'few Saxon drying kilns have been excavated' by 1975 (page 33). This is no longer the case, with abundant examples of varying size and shape having been excavated across the country, dating almost exclusively from the later 7th century onwards (e.g. Carver 2010; Hardy et al. 2007; Heaton 1993; Hinton and Peacock 2020). One especially noteworthy recent discovery is an elaborate malting complex of eighth- to ninth-century date at Sedgeford in Norfolk, the earliest such complex so far found in Anglo-Saxon England (Faulkner and Blakelock 2020). In my own research, I have undertaken a regional survey of some of the evidence for the 7th-9th centuries (McKerracher 2018: 76–79), but nothing approaching a national synthesis for the entire Anglo-Saxon period has been attempted. To the best of my knowledge, the same is true of the whole medieval period in England.

It thus remains that, in terms of geographical and chronological scope, Rickett's study is still unequalled. On the other hand, the huge and growing datasets now available have rendered such a wide-ranging survey impractical (Rickett had 58 entries in his gazetteer; Comeau and Burrow have now identified 148 in Wales alone). Radiocarbon dating has also become more routine and precise since 1975, meaning that we can gain a much clearer chronological perspective than was possible when Rickett completed his study. Challenges for future research therefore include not only the periodic updating of regional and national gazetteers, but also continuing inter-regional and international comparisons, the development of shared and consistent terminology, and a rigorous and evolving approach to interpretation. In these endeavours, we may follow the example of Mr Rickett.

Post-Roman and Medieval Drying Kilns

Robert Rickett (1975)

In 1886, General Pitt-Rivers found a number of structures, which he interpreted as hypocausts, in his excavations of the Romano-British village at Rushmore, on Woodcuts Common in Cranborne Chase, Dorset (Pitt-Rivers 1887). It was not until 1912, however, that the real function of these and similar structures was realised by Professor Gowland, in an appendix to the report on the structures found at the Hambleden villa in Buckinghamshire: 'In my opinion, they are the flues of drying-floors which have been used for drying harvested grain' (Cocks 1921). In 1943, Mr R.G. Goodchild published an examination of several T-shaped corn drying kilns together with a suggested reconstruction of their drying floors, based on his discoveries at Atworth, Wiltshire (Goodchild 1943). Since then, many other Roman T-shaped drying kilns have been excavated in the British Isles, as well as many other types of drying kiln and large drying floors, such as at Great Casterton, Rutland (Corder 1954), and Old Sleaford, Lincolnshire (Wilson 1961). In light of all this new evidence, a new assessment of the Roman drying kilns is needed.

Meanwhile, post-medieval corn drying kilns have been discussed by Sir Lindsay Scott, together with some evidence for kilns of earlier periods (Scott 1951). Several regional studies of post-medieval and fairly recent kilns have also been made, and derelict and abandoned kilns in some areas have been recorded (Ramm *et al.* 1972), but much fieldwork still remains to be done.

This book attempts to go some way to fill the gap between these Roman and post-medieval reviews, and to provide a basis for future studies. The book covers the post-Roman and medieval periods, but the exact chronological limits are not closely defined. Drying kilns which have been dated to the early post-Roman period, but which are obviously of Roman type, have been omitted – for instance, the two L-shaped corn drying kilns excavated at Hereford (Selkirk and Selkirk 1968a). These can be paralleled on other Roman sites such as Mancetter (Wilson 1966), West Blatchington (Norris and Burstow 1950), and Longthorpe (Wild 1973). At the other end of the period, kilns of the 16th century are included in this study, but those of the 17th century are omitted. All dates are AD unless stated otherwise.

All of the post-Roman and medieval kilns (or groups of kilns) which form the basis of this study are compiled in the Gazetteer at the end of the book, which includes further details about each entry. Each kiln or site in the Gazetteer has been assigned a 'K' number, and they are identified by these numbers throughout the main text, e.g. Faxton (**K10**). The kilns are classified into Types I to VII, with additional categories for those considered unclassifiable or not deemed to be drying kilns: the rationale and typology are set out in the Gazetteer (page 39). The characteristics of these kilns are summarised in Table 1, and their distribution is shown in Figures 1-3.

Table 1 - Summary of characteristics of the kilns in the Gazetteer.

gaz. no.	site name	kiln type	F/B	AG/BG	evidence of function	evidence of fuel	published interpretation	my interp.
K1	Stamford kiln 1	IA	B	BG	grain	burnt wood, twigs, ash	MK	DK
K2	Stamford kiln 2	IA	?B	BG	-	-	CDK	DK
K3	Stamford kiln 3	IA	B	BG	-	burnt wood, twigs, black and grey ash	CDK	DK
K4	Great Casterton	IB	?F	BG	mainly barley	-	MK	DK
K5	Montgomery Castle	IB	-	BG	-	-	?TK	DK
K6	Stamford kiln 4	IB	?F	BG	-	burnt wood, black ash, twigs	DK	DK
K7	Barrow	IIA	B	BG	-	-	MK	DK
K8	Grafton Regis	IIA	B	AG	barley, oats	charcoal, ash, burnt wood	MK	MK
K9	Brixworth	IIB	?F	BG	-	-	MK	DK
K10	Faxton	IIB	F	?AG	peas, bean seeds	-	DK	DK
K11	Nottingham Caves (6 kilns)	IIIA	caves	BG	-	-	CDKs/MKs	DKs
K12	Rue Farm	IIIA	B	BG	grain husks	black ash	CDK	DK
K13	Sandal Castle	IIIA	B	BG	grain	-	MK	MK
K14	Doncaster	IIIB	?F	BG	-	-	MK	DK
K15	Nottingham (8 kilns)	IIIB	?F?B	BG	one with grain	-	CDKs/MKs/other	DKs

gaz. no.	site name	kiln type	F/B	AG/BG	evidence of function	evidence of fuel	published interpretation	my interp.
K16	Stanhope	IIIB	?F	BG	-	black ash	CDK	DK
K17	Alcester	IVA	?B	BG	-	charcoal	DK	DK
K18	Houndtor (2 kilns)	IVA	B	AG	-	ash, charcoal in both	CDKs	DKs
K19	South Witham (2 kilns)	IVA	B	-	grain in both	-	MKs	?MKs
K20	Ballymacash	IVB	-	-	-	-	?CDK	?
K21	Beere (2 kilns)	IVB	F	BG	-	ashes of brushwood/undergrowth in one	CDK	DK
K22	Glenvoidean	IVB	F	BG	-	-	CDK	DK
K23	Rathbeg	IVB	F	BG	-	charcoal	flax/CDK	DK
K24	Sandal Castle	IVB	F	?BG	-	-	CDK	DK
K25	St. Blane's	IVB	F	BG	-	-	CDK	DK
K26	Buckden	IVC	F	BG	-	-	?baking or CDK	DK
K27	Glen Parva	IVC	F	BG	-	sooty material, grey ash	?DK	DK
K28	Jarlshof (2 kilns)	V	B	AG	-	-	CDKs	DKs
K29	Kirkstall Abbey	V	B	AG	-	-	MK	?MK
K30	Stretham	V	B	AG	barley	-	CDK	?MK
K31	Ballycatteen	VI	F	BG	-	bright red soil (?peat ash)	DK, ?flax	DK
K32	Doarlish Cashen	VIIA	F	BG	-	wood, peat ash	?CDK	?

gaz. no.	site name	kiln type	F/B	AG/BG	evidence of function	evidence of fuel	published interpretation	my interp.
K33	Highlight	VIIA	F	AG	grain	straw, brushwood, small twigs	CDK	DK
K34	Hullasey	VIIA	?F	BG	-	-	?CDK	?
K35	Letterkeen	VIIA	F	BG	-	charcoal, red ash	?CDK	?
K36	Lundy Island	VIIA	B	-	-	-	?CDK	?fireplace
K37	Uisneach	VIIA	?F	?AG	-	-	?CDK	?
K38	Underhoull	VIIA	?B	AG	-	-	?CDK	?
K39	Altmush	VIIB	-	BG	-	-	CDK	DK
K40	Garranes	VIIB	F	AG	-	-	?CDK	?
K41	Michelham Priory (2 kilns)	VIIB	B	AG	-	ash, burnt wood in shared flue	?CDKs	?
K42	Tintagel	VIIB	B	AG	-	-	CDK	?
K43	Merthyr Dyfan	VIIB	-	-	-	-	?	?
K44	Alcester	-	F	-	-	-	DK	?
K45	Block Eary	-	F	BG	-	peat ash	?CDK	?
K46	Deddington Castle	-	B	-	-	-	DK	?
K47	Inishkea North	-	?F	-	-	-	DK	DK
K48	Lincoln (several kilns)	-	-	-	-	-	DK's	?
K49	Northampton (2 kilns)	-	-	BG	-	-	malt ovens	?

gaz. no.	site name	kiln type	F/B	AG/BG	evidence of function	evidence of fuel	published interpretation	my interp.
K50	Rhuddlan	-	-	-	-	-	meat, fish drying	?
K51	Scole	-	-	BG	-	-	?CDK	?
K52	Spaunton New Inn	-	-	-	-	-	?	?
K53	Sutton	-	-	-	-	-	CDK	?
K54	Thetford (several kilns)	-	-	-	-	-	CDKs	?
K55	Wallingford Castle (2 kilns)	-	-	-	wheat and rye in both	-	CD ovens	DKs
K56	Fountains Abbey	? II/V	B	-	-	-	MK	vat emp.; MK
K57	Stamford	-	-	-	-	-	DK	large oven
K58	Winchester	-	-	-	-	-	MK	lime kiln

Key

AG – above ground

BG – (partly) below ground

CDK – corn drying kiln

DK – drying kiln

F – free-standing

B – in a building

MK – malt kiln

TK – tile kiln

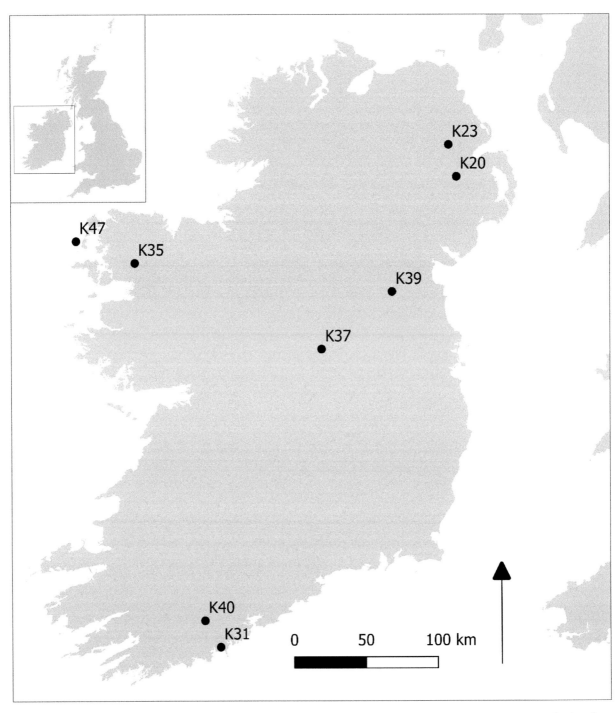

Figure 1 - Distribution of kilns/sites in the Gazetteer on the island of Ireland. Great Britain and islands boundary data from Ordnance Survey Open Data © Crown copyright and database right 2017, under the Open Government licence. Isle of Man boundary data from Hijmans *et al.* 2015 under Attribution 3.0 Unported licence (https://creativecommons.org/licenses/by/3.0, viewed 29 June 2021). Island of Ireland boundary data from *Irish Townlands* (https://www.townlands.ie, viewed 29 June 2021) using OpenStreetMap data © OpenStreetMap contributors, under the Open Data Commons Open Database licence (http://opendatacommons.org/licenses/odbl, viewed 29 June 2021).

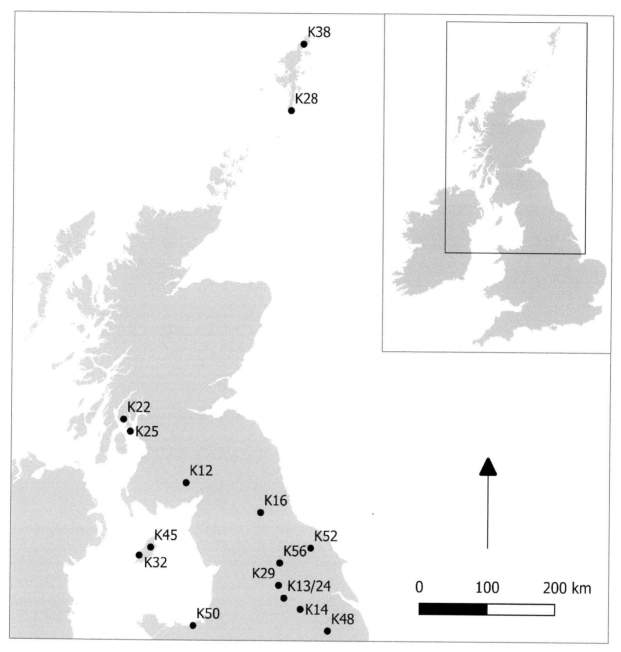

Figure 2 - Distribution of kilns/sites in the Gazetteer in northern Britain, the Shetland Islands and the Isle of Man. Great Britain and islands boundary data from Ordnance Survey Open Data © Crown copyright and database right 2017, under the Open Government licence. Isle of Man boundary data from Hijmans *et al.* 2015 under Attribution 3.0 Unported licence (https://creativecommons.org/licenses/by/3.0, viewed 29 June 2021). Island of Ireland boundary data from *Irish Townlands* (https://www.townlands.ie, viewed 29 June 021) using OpenStreetMap data © OpenStreetMap contributors, under the Open Data Commons Open Database licence (http://opendatacommons.org/licenses/odbl, viewed 29 June 2021).

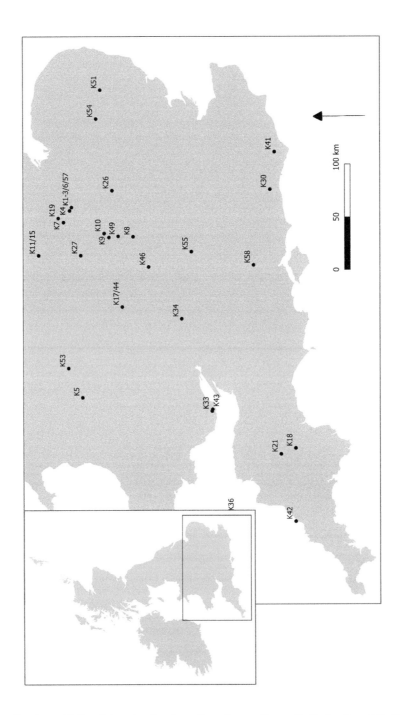

Figure 3 - Distribution of kilns/sites in the Gazetteer in southern Britain. Great Britain and islands boundary data from Ordnance Survey Open Data © Crown copyright and database right 2017, under the Open Government licence. Isle of Man boundary data from Hijmans *et al.* 2015 under Attribution 3.0 Unported licence (https://creativecommons.org/licenses/by/3.0, viewed 29 June 2021). Island of Ireland boundary data from *Irish Townlands* (https://www.townlands.ie, viewed 29 June 2021) using OpenStreetMap data © OpenStreetMap contributors, under the Open Data Commons Open Database licence (http://opendatacommons.org/licenses/odbl, viewed 29 June 2021).

Identifying drying kilns in archaeology

Many structures are found, either in buildings or free-standing, which are interpreted as drying kilns by their very nature. Some of these drying kilns have their lower part built into the ground, or into banks or slopes, mainly to support the sides; others are built entirely above the ground, either adjoining buildings or surrounded by stone platforms. Some are built of stone, some of stone and clay. A kiln with sides of wattling coated with clay is known from Nottingham (**K15**). Others are completely rock-cut, while in some a rock-cut edge has been used as part of the structure.

The majority of drying kilns possess a drying chamber, a flue and a stoking area. The drying chamber, above which was placed the drying floor, is either square or rectangular, circular or oval, with or without battered sides, and with a more or less flat floor. The flue, a defined channel of varying length, leads into the drying chamber. The fire was lit within the flue, and its position can be deduced from signs of heating and burning on the sides and floor of the flue. Where the fire was close to the opening into the drying chamber, the need to protect the drying floor from flames and sparks was met by the use of a baffle stone (e.g. Stamford kiln 4; **K6**), or some other expedient. In other kilns, the fire was some distance away from the drying chamber, at the mouth of the flue, which may be covered with flagstones along its entire length. Outside the mouth of the flue was the stoking area, which in some cases was defined to form a stokehole. In other cases, the fire, just inside the mouth of the flue, was attended from an undefined stoking area.

Exceptions do occur, such as those kilns which had only a drying chamber, at the base of which a fire was lit, and the drying floor was placed over the top; this may have been the case in the Altmush kiln (**K39**). In other cases, the commodity to be dried was placed on the flagstones covering the flue or flues, such as in the Ballycatteen kiln (**K31**).

It is evident that only a gentle heat was required in the drying chamber where, in some kilns with battered sides, the heat was fanned out below the drying floor. In other cases, the source of heat was some distance away from the drying chamber. Thus, the arrangement of these kilns rules out other functions such as baking or the firing of earthenware, which require a more intense heat which is retained within the kiln.

Some drying kilns are identified as such on the basis that a fire had left ashes but had not burnt the flue heavily, if at all, therefore no great heat had been required (e.g. those at Beere: **K21**). However, in the larger kilns the fire needed to be more intense in order to heat the large drying floors (e.g. Stamford kiln 3: **K3**). Thus the intensity of the fire is related to the size of the kiln and the drying floor, as well as the distance between the fire and the drying chamber.

That these kilns functioned successfully seems obvious from their continued use, in more or less the same form, through many centuries. Many medieval kilns resemble very closely post-medieval and modern drying kilns and, in some cases, Roman drying kilns too. This can be seen in the following comparisons.

(A) Kilns with steps down to defined stoking area:

- fourth-century kilns at Thundersbarrow Hill, West Sussex (Figure 4; Curwen 1933);
- thirteenth- or fourteenth-century kiln 3 at Stamford (**K3**; Figure 20);
- late eighteenth- or early nineteenth-century kiln at Well, North Yorkshire (Gilyard-Beer 1951) (Figure 5);
- mid-nineteenth-century kiln which stood outside the King's Mill in Stamford, Lincolnshire (Figures 6-7).

(B) Drying kilns at the end of barns:

- the thirteenth-century drying kilns at the end of the barns at Houndtor (**K18**);
- the eighteenth- or nineteenth-century corn drying kilns at Peninerine and Griminish in the Outer Hebrides, which are typical of many in Scotland and the Outer Islands (Figure 8; Whitaker 1957).

(C) Roughly keyhole-shaped kilns with unenclosed stoking areas:

- twelfth- to thirteenth-century free-standing kilns at Beere (**K21**);
- many similar post-medieval kilns, for example that at Emlagh, Co. Cork (Figure 9; Ó Ríordáin and Foy 1941).

(D) Kilns adjoining barns:

- fourteenth- to fifteenth-century kilns adjoining a building at Jarlshof (**K28**);
- many post-medieval and modern corn drying kilns adjoining barns, typical of Scotland and the Outer Islands (Jamieson 1968).

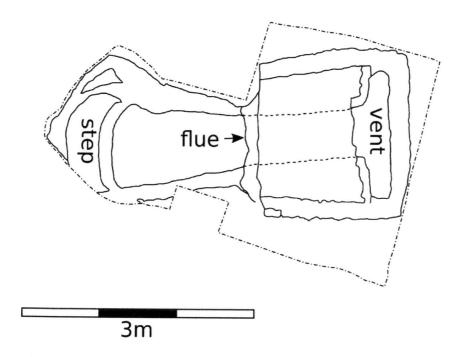

3m

Figure 4 – Plan of Romano-British kiln at Thundersbarrow Hill (after Curwen 1933 Plate XX).

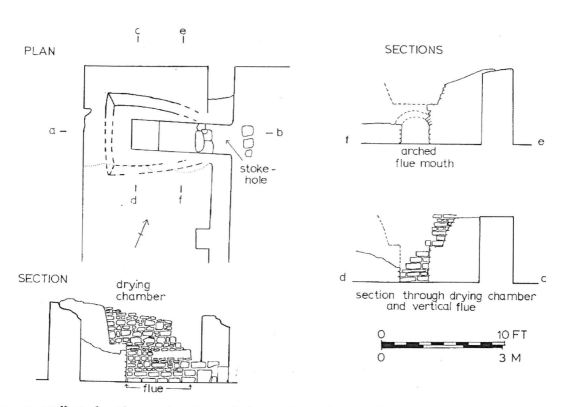

Figure 5 - Well, Yorks: Plans and sections of a late eighteenth- or early nineteenth-century drying kiln in the ruins of the Roman bath-house (after Gilyard-Beer 1951).

Figure 6 - Mid-nineteenth century corn drying kiln at the King's Mill, Stamford during demolition. Reproduced by kind permission of the *Rutland & Stamford Mercury*.

Figure 7 - Mid-nineteenth century corn drying kiln at the King's Mill, Stamford during demolition. Reproduced by kind permission of the *Rutland & Stamford Mercury*.

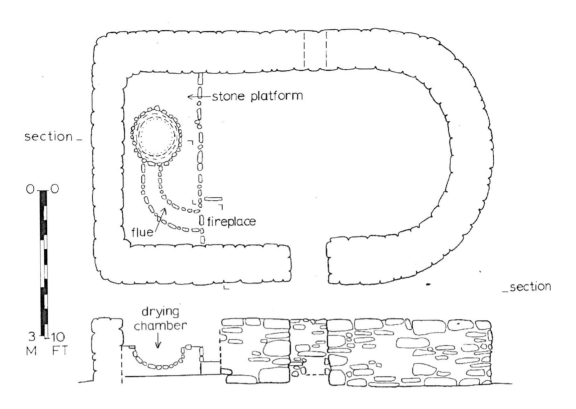

Figure 8 - Peninerine, South Uist, Outer Hebrides: Plan and section of eighteenth- or nineteenth-century drying kiln in a barn (after Mr Whitaker).

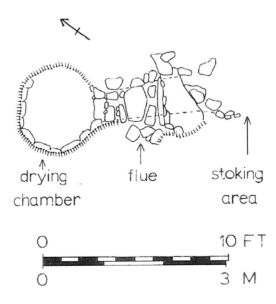

Figure 9 - Emlagh, Co. Cork, post-medieval drying kiln (after Ó Ríordáin and Foy 1941).

Many kilns of similar form to excavated medieval examples were in use until the 19th century, and folk memories exist of exactly how they were used.

The interpretation of excavated structures as drying kilns based on their plans can be strengthened by the discovery of grain or some other commodity either on the floor of the drying chamber or scattered around the kiln from when the chamber was cleaned out. In the former case, the grains or other remains must have arrived there by the accidental burning and collapse of the drying floor (or 'kiln hair': see page 30), resulting in the charring of the commodity upon it; or as a result of small particles slipping through the drying floor when the crop was placed upon it or during its subsequent turning whilst being dried. In malting, the chafings which fell down through the kiln hair or drying floor were known as 'kiln dust', and this was regularly cleaned out (Wright 1923: 'kiln').

Some structures which have been found and interpreted as drying kilns have no parallels and offer no clear evidence of their function. Some may indeed be drying kilns, but technological experimentation undoubtedly took place, and some simple structures may have served many purposes including the drying of grains and other commodities.

Certain drying kilns have a specific function: if they are found within brewhouses or malthouses, for example, they might logically be called malting kilns. However, grain drying and malting were not only practised in specialised drying kilns. In post-medieval times, grain was dried over the domestic hearth, in small quantities, as and when it was needed, and there is no reason why this practice should not have occurred in the post-Roman and medieval periods as well (see page 102).

At Bolton Castle, North Yorkshire, the fourteenth-century brewhouse and bakehouse were combined (Jackson 1956). The existence of a malting room on the floor above would suggest that the drying of malt was carried out in the baking ovens. In the early 17th century, when home brewing was on the increase, bakehouse ovens were used for the drying of malt (Barley 1961). This trend started in the late medieval period: in the will of John Cocksedge of Felsham, Suffolk, who died in 1467, a 'bakehouse for baking and drying of malt' is mentioned (Barley 1961). This does not mean, however, that bakehouse ovens can be considered as drying kilns. A drying kiln must be defined as a structure which has been specially designed, built and originally used for the drying of some commodity.

Evidence of function

The Gazetteer has 58 entries for which drying kiln functions have been suggested by the excavators or other writers. Some of these consist of more than one structure, so the total is 72 at least (two entries just state 'several'). Of these, 52 can be identified as certain or probable drying kilns (see above, Table 1, 'my interpretation'). 15 of these have produced evidence for a particular function on the basis of information available to date (see above, Table 1, 'evidence of function'). The other 37 can be considered consistent with a drying kiln interpretation because of their form and construction.

What kinds of evidence are present in those 15 cases? For some, this evidence is in the form of carbonised grain, husks and seeds found within or associated with the kilns. Grain has been found in 12 kilns, identified as wheat and rye in two kilns at Wallingford Castle (**K55**); as barley and oats at Grafton Regis (**K8**); and barley at Great Casterton (**K4**) and Stretham (**K30**). Unspecified types of grain or grain husks were found in kilns at Stamford (**K1**), Rue Farm (**K12**), Sandal Castle (**K13**), in one of the kilns at Nottingham (**K15**), in both kilns at South Witham (**K19**), and at Highlight (**K33**). At Faxton (**K10**), a preliminary identification has revealed the seeds of peas and beans.

This total of 15 kilns includes two which are probably malting kilns due to their position in malt- or brewhouses, at Kirkstall Abbey (**K29**) and Fountains Abbey (**K56**). At Fountains Abbey, the structure at the north end of the building, published as a malt kiln, is more likely to be a heated vat emplacement or boiler. However, in the southwest corner is a rectangular structure which is probably a malting kiln.

However, it would be naïve to believe that such kilns were only used to dry that particular commodity indicated by the surviving remains. The accumulation of ash, carbonised grain, husks, and shoots of malted grain in a kiln would have been cleared out at intervals. Thus the remains found may only be representative of the use of the kiln since the last clearing-out. Furthermore, it is possible that certain commodities dried in a kiln may not have left any surviving remains.

Other functions, and relationship of kiln type to function

Some kilns were probably originally built to serve a particular purpose, such as malting. However, they may well have been used to dry other commodities in between episodes of malting. Other kilns would probably have been intended from the outset to dry a range of different things. Also, it is difficult to argue that drying kilns of a certain form have specific functions, and the limitations of this means of interpretation must be recognised, as in many cases positive evidence is lacking.

The kiln at Ballycatteen (**K31**) is remarkably similar in form to a nineteenth-century flax drying kiln at Meenanea, Co. Tyrone, and to many other flax drying kilns in that county (Figure 10; Davies 1938). They have an unusual plan, and it is tempting to suggest that this is related to their specific function. However, Ballycatteen is in the south of Ireland, and Co. Tyrone in the north, and the kilns may have served different purposes in different regions. Ballycatteen is also earlier in date, and although the basic form of the kiln remained unchanged, it does not follow that the use to which the later kilns were put has also remained unchanged. Furthermore, flax drying in Ireland in post-medieval times was not limited to this type of kiln, as in other regions it was also dried on other types of kiln, one of which is similar to kilns used for corn drying (Evans 1957). A similarly variable situation may also have existed in earlier times.

BALLYCATTEEN

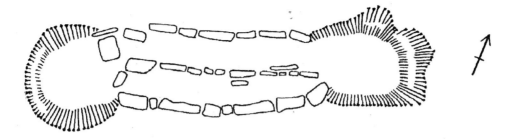

MEENANEA

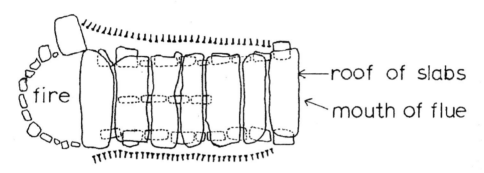

roof of slabs

mouth of flue

fire

0   10 FT

0   3 M

Figure 10 - A comparison of a drying kiln at Ballycatteen, Co. Cork, and a nineteenth-century flax-drying kiln at Meenanea, Co. Tyrone.

The same is true of malting kilns: several types were used. Those with circular drying chambers occur at Sandal Castle (**K13**), South Witham (**K19**), Stretham (**K30**) and Kirkstall Abbey (**K29**), but those at Grafton Regis (**K8**) and Great Casterton (**K4**) have rectangular drying chambers. These are just broad differences which would become greater if other aspects of these kilns were to be examined. In fairly recent times, malting was carried out in kilns built much earlier for the drying of corn. In the Hebrides, for instance, corn drying kilns in barns were once re-used for the illicit preparation of malt for whisky distilling (Mercer 1972); and some free-standing corn kilns in Ireland were put to similar use (Evans 1945).

Kilns which do not seem to be associated with a malt- or brew-house may still have been used for malting, especially perhaps if barley grains have been found within them. This was probably the function of the kiln at Great Casterton (**K4**), as it was close to the church, and may have been used by the church authorities for malting (see page 37). However, barley was probably the chief grain used for bread in continental Europe as late as the 16th century (*Encyclopædia Britannica*: 'barley'). In fairly recent times, bere (a six-rowed barley) was grown in the far north of Scotland, and kiln-dried to make scones or bannocks (Jamieson 1968); and in the Isle of Man, barley was kiln-dried to make meal (Cubbon and Megaw 1969). Thus, the discovery of barley grains in a kiln may not always indicate malting. It must also be remembered that barley was not the only grain used for malting, although it was preferred if possible (see page 23).

Many drying kilns, such as that at Faxton (**K10**), were probably multi-purpose. This would have been the case with kilns owned communally, and also with those owned by the Lord of the Manor or by a private individual (see pages 35-36). Thus a variety of crops, and perhaps other things, would have been dried upon them. Regionalism and cultural traditions must be taken into account when considering what sort of crops would have been dried upon a particular kiln, since different grain crops were grown in different regions. 'Corn' is only a general term for the grain crops characteristic of each geographical region (*Encyclopædia Britannica*: 'corn'), and the description of many kilns as 'corn drying kilns' may not cover all their possible uses.

This is supported by the documentary evidence. Besides many references to corn drying and malting, there are sixteenth-century references to the kiln-drying of hops and beans; and there is a reference of 1577 to the drying of chives (that is, the stigma of the saffron plant, or autumn crocus, dried for use as a dye) in a small kiln covered with 'streined canvasses' (Murray 1888: 'kiln' and 'kiln-dry'). A similar situation existed in the post-medieval period: there are references to the kiln drying not only of oats and wheat but also potatoes (Wright 1923: 'kiln') and lumber (Whitney 1899: 'kiln').

Other commodities of the post-Roman and medieval periods would have required kiln drying: flax and hemp are known to have been grown in the Midlands (Hoskins 1965), and in other areas as well; fish and meat needed drying or smoking if they were not cured by other means. A kiln at Rhuddlan (**K50**) had been used for drying fish and meat on a commercial scale, but it is not known on what evidence this interpretation was based. A variety of other things may have required kiln drying at some stage: bracken, faggots, hay and straw are possibilities, and the drying of withies has been suggested (S. Taylor pers. comm.); pottery must not be excluded, as this is known to have been kiln dried in the Roman period at the Oxford potteries (Young 1972), and is also suggested (K.F. Hartley pers. comm.) for a large drying kiln at Mancetter (Wilson 1966).

Purposes of kiln drying
Corn was kiln-dried for several different purposes: as a preliminary to threshing or grinding, or to prevent germination during storage.

In those areas where the lack of sunlight and the damp climate prevented the crop from fully ripening before it was harvested, it was necessary to dry the incompletely hardened grain before threshing. This is a practice which still survives on the farms in the Faeroes, and until recent times corn kilns were still being used in the west from the Shetlands to Ireland and Wales (Evans 1957; Fenton 1963; Jamieson 1968; Scott 1951). However, in the late medieval period, with the climatic deterioration of the 14th and 15th centuries, the drying of crops may have been necessary in the lowland areas of Britain. With the climatic optimum of the 12th and 13th centuries and increased demand for agricultural land in the 13th century, much more marginal land came under cultivation (Hurst and Beresford 1971: 115). At some settlements where this took place, such as Houndtor (**K18**) and Beere (**K21**), it may have been difficult to dry the crops naturally, and so there was a need for drying kilns. In cases such as these, it may be that the use of drying kilns enabled the land to be cultivated at all.

The normal purpose of kiln drying was to harden the grain for grinding. Before the introduction of the power driven mills with kilns, the corn was stored in ricks for preservation, and dried just before grinding, which was done mainly with hand querns (Cubbon and Megaw 1969; Evans 1957; Scott 1951). The purpose of many of the post-Roman and medieval kilns would have been to harden the grain before grinding (the advantages of this have been stated by Curwen 1938: 151–152). The presence of querns and quern fragments close to the kiln at Inishkea North (**K47**), the possible kiln at Letterkeen (**K35**), and in the kiln at Highlight (**K34**), is significant in this respect. During some periods in the Middle Ages, people were forbidden to grind their own flour in hand querns and had to use the manorial mill (see pages 35-36).

Drying kilns were also used in the malting process. Large quantities of ale were produced in brewhouses until the late medieval period, when the introduction of hops from Flanders enabled beer to be brewed (see page 37). Any cereal grain can be converted to malt by the germination of rye, wheat or oats, or a mixture of different grains, but barley was considered to be the best (Salzman 1913; *Encyclopædia Britannica*: 'malt').

The barley was first put in a large lead cistern and steeped in water to make it swell, then it was spread on the malting floor to germinate. It was regularly raked, over a number of weeks, to ensure uniform growth. When it had germinated sufficiently, it was put on a kiln to dry, spread about 0.08 m thick on a hair cloth over a wooden frame. Straw was considered the best fuel for malt kilns, but fern or wood were also used. The drying burnt off the shoots, arresting the growth of the barley, and converted it into malt. The process took from one to four days, depending on the type of malt required; and this also determined the heat of the fire (Steer 1969). It was periodically turned during drying, with malt shovels and forks. The barley was then ground and used to brew ale or beer, for which coppers for boiling and vats for cooling and fermenting were needed (Brakspear 1905; Steer 1969).

Malting kilns occur in the malt- and brew-houses at Kirkstall Abbey (**K29**), Grafton Regis (**K8**), Sandal Castle (**K13**), Stretham (**K30**), probably at Fountains Abbey (**K56**), and in the possible brewhouse at South Witham (**K19**). In many other cases, the malt was presumably prepared in the baking oven as, for example, at Bolton Castle in North Yorkshire (Jackson 1956) and Lindisfarne Priory on Holy Island (Hamilton-Thompson 1949). The bread oven would also have been used for making malt in smaller households (Salzman 1926).

Some of the drying kilns found in the towns may have been attached to brewhouses, to produce malted grain for use in brewing ale or beer, which were sold in the alehouses (see pages 36-37). This may have been the function of some of the kilns found at Nottingham (**K15**), and perhaps also of Stamford kilns 1 and 4 (**K1, K6**).

Hemp and flax were important crops in the Middle Ages, when housewives spun and wove their own linen (Salzman 1926). The process of flax preparation is described in the early Christian Irish laws, notably in the Brehon Law (Joyce 1903). After pulling, the flax was tied up in sheaves and dried. It was then steeped or retted in water to rot the woody fibre. It was then kiln-dried, so that the brittle woody covering of the flax fibre could be broken up with a mallet. This was then removed by hand in a process called 'scutching'. The 'hackling' process then divided the fibres into finer filaments for spinning into thread, which, after further treatment, was woven into linen.

Other crops, such as peas, beans and chives would probably have been kiln-dried to preserve them; and the drying of fish and meat would have been useful for preservation, although deliberate smoking of these two commodities must not be ruled out.

Evidence of fuel

Of the 52 certain or probable drying kilns (see above, Table 1, 'my interpretation'), 14 have produced evidence of the type of fuel used (see above, Table 1, 'evidence of fuel'). Descriptions vary considerably and many are only preliminary, in the absence of specialist identifications. As 'ash' is rather unspecific, it has been omitted from Table 1 and the total above, since it could be derived from various sources – fuel, a burnt kiln floor, or a commodity burnt accidentally during drying. The interpretation will depend upon its composition and position within the kiln. The fuel remains found may be representative of the fuel used for one commodity during several kiln loads, or the remains might be an accumulation of the fuel used for several different commodities. In some cases a mixture of fuels may have been used for a single episode of drying.

In most cases, the fuel used would have depended upon what was available in the locality at that time. If, however, a choice was available, then this would depend on the commodity to be dried, and the size and form of the kiln. In post-medieval times, some Shetlanders recognised that the smoke of peat fuel, when used for drying, added to the flavour of bere (barley) meal, but detracted from the flavour of oat meal (Jamieson 1968). Straw was considered to be the best fuel for malting, but fern or wood were also used. The type of fuel used for malting barley often added additional flavours to the drink; for example, malt intended for Scotch whisky is dried over a fire to which peat is added (*Encyclopædia Britannica*: 'malt'). The heat generated by the fire, and the length of drying, were also determined by the type of malt required. This was undoubtedly recognised in the Middle Ages: there was a saying, current in 1546, that 'soft fire maketh sweete malte' (Murray 1888: 'malt').

Remains of wood have been found in a number of cases. Small twigs, partly burnt, were found in Stamford kilns 1, 3 and 4 (**K1, K3, K6**), at Grafton Regis (**K8**), and at Highlight (**K33**). Elsewhere, charcoal and wood ash have been found. Grey ash and black ash, noted in several cases, may represent wood and straw. In Stamford kiln 3 (**K3**), a small layer of red and grey ash was interleaved in black ash with burnt twigs, probably indicating the use of different fuels at different stages.

Faggots of straw, bound by withies, were probably used, as they were in the post-medieval period. Perhaps the small twigs found in some ash deposits are the remains of these withies. Straw was found at Highlight (**K33**), along with small twigs and brushwood. Straw, furze and brushwood shower sparks, and thus necessitate some form of protection for the drying floor. Long-flued kilns are a response to this (Scott 1951: 203), such as the one at Rue Farm (**K12**), where large quantities of black ash were found outside the flue. Different expedients were employed in other kilns, such as baffle stones like the one found in Stamford kiln 4 (**K6**).

Peat was used extensively to fire kilns in the north and west of the British Isles, as it was readily available and plentiful. The characteristic red ash has been found in the kilns at Doarlish Cashen (**K32**), Letterkeen (**K35**) and possibly at Ballycatteen (**K31**). In other areas turf fuel was probably used.

Other things were probably used as fuel, such as the waste and chaff from threshing and winnowing. Coal was not used because of the unpleasant taste it would have given to the grain; it was not used until the introduction of smokeless Welsh coal in the later post-medieval period (Steer 1969). Cinders were found in the kiln at St Blane's (**K25**), but these may have been formed by the embers of successive straw fires, mixed with earth, which was used to dampen the fire, and became hardened with each successive firing. Such a deposit, resembling clinker, was found in the possible drying kiln at Castlehill Wood Dun, Stirlingshire (Feachem 1957).

Siting, and materials and methods of construction

Some kilns may have been sited with regard to the prevailing wind direction, but this is difficult to prove. In many cases other factors were probably more important, and the kiln would then have been used on days when the wind was in such a direction as to assist the convection of hot air through the drying floor. In assessing the importance of such factors, the siting of several kilns in a small, localised area must be studied, for instance the kilns at Nottingham (**K15**) or those in Stamford. Kiln 4 at Stamford (**K6**) was aligned east-west, with the drying chamber at the west end; kilns 1, 2 and 3 were all aligned roughly north-south (**K1, K2, K3**). However, the drying chamber of kiln 1, in the town, was at the north end, whereas kilns 2 and 3, in the castle bailey, were both built with the drying chamber at the south end. Thus, it would seem that the prevailing wind direction had little influence on siting, but one does not know whether this changed during a century or so. It must also be borne in mind that the wind direction in built-up places would have varied over small areas.

Several kilns were built into banks and slopes for stability, as the flue was much lower than the top of the battered sides of the drying chambers (Figure 14). The kiln at Stanhope (**K16**) was built in this way; that at Rathbeg (**K23**) was built in what would originally have been the inner slope of the rath bank; those at Beere (**K21**) and Rue Farm (**K12**) were built into slopes; and that at Glenvoidean (**K22**) was built into the side of a prehistoric burial cairn. Many post-medieval kilns made use of banks and slopes, whether man-made or natural, in this way (Feachem 1957). The flue, covered by flagstones, ran from the foot of the bank, underground to the base of the drying chamber. Thus, the siting, in some cases, was dependent upon the landscape.

Some of the kilns surviving today had a large proportion of their lower parts constructed below the contemporary ground surface. Most of the kilns of Types I to IV needed support for the sides and were therefore built in this way; but those at Houndtor (**K18**) and Grafton Regis (**K8**) were surrounded by stone platforms. Parts of others built on the contemporary ground surface, such as those of Type V and that at Highlight (**K33**), survive to varying heights. Greater or lesser parts of kilns survive, depending on the amount of disturbance since they became disused; the remains of the kiln at Buckden (**K26**), for instance, are very fragmentary. The materials used in the construction of the probable kiln at Glen Parva (**K27**) do not survive; all that is left is the bottom part of the trench cut into the natural. Other drying kilns built on the contemporary ground surface may have been totally destroyed since the Middle Ages. Temporary structures (see page 36) would have left little archaeological trace, perhaps only a patch of burning. Those built of turf may also leave scant remains; the post-medieval flax drying kilns characteristic of Co. Armagh were described as 'small sod buildings left open at the top... built by the sides of fences near the cabins: they are four or five feet in diameter and have a hurdle of sticks placed across them at a convenient height (about four feet), on which a small quantity of flax is spread to dry over a turf fire' (Evans 1957).

Some medieval kilns utilised rock-cut edges as part of their structure, such as the east side of the stokehole at Great Casterton (**K4**), which was cut from the natural ironstone. Others were completely rock-cut, such as Spaunton New Inn (**K52**), and some of the Nottingham kilns (**K15**) which were cut into the surface deposits and the Bunter Sandstone. The Nottingham cave kilns (**K11**) were cut into the underground rock, but kiln IIIB at the Drury Hill site had a stone-lined stokehole in its second phase.

Stone was the most common material used to build these kilns. This was local stone, either from quarries or re-used from other stone structures. All of the Stamford kilns were built of local limestone; kiln 3 (**K3**) also had some ironstone and Collyweston slate, and kiln 4 (**K6**) had some sandstone and Barnack Rag. The Great Casterton kiln (**K4**) was mainly built of limestone, but with some ironstone; the Faxton kiln was built of ironstone (**K10**); that at Brixworth was built of ferruginous sandstone (**K9**); and

Arden Sandstone was used for the kiln found at Alcester in 1968-9 (**K17**). The quality of building varies; the stonework of the Stamford kilns was neat and laid with care, whereas that of other structures, such as St Blane's (**K25**), was crudely put together. The kilns at Beere (**K21**) and Highlight (**K33**) were of drystone construction, and that at Rathbeg (**K23**) was built of boulders and clay. Elsewhere the stones were set into the clay and earth of the banks and slopes into which they were built, such as in the Stanhope kiln (**K16**). In many kilns, there is little evidence for the use of mortar. At Stretham, however, the foundation course consisted of sharp flints in white mortar, over which were laid ironstone boulders in clay (**K30**).

The floors of many kilns consisted of the natural into which they were constructed; some, however, had stone laid upon them, perhaps to prevent erosion by the cleaning out of ashes. The floor of the flue and drying chamber of Stamford kiln 3 was covered by Collyweston slate surrounded by stone, but the floor of the stokehole was formed of the natural with clay over it in parts (**K3**). Part of the floor of the drying chamber and the stokehole floor of Stamford kiln 1 were covered with plaster (**K1**); the flue and part of the drying chamber of the Brixworth kiln were covered with limestone (**K9**); and the flue and drying chamber of the Jarlshof kiln were partially flagged (**K28**). The stokehole of the Barrow kiln may originally have had a planked wooden floor (**K7**). Some floors were sloping, such as in Stamford kilns 1, 2 and 3 (**K1**, **K2**, **K3**) and that at Great Casterton (**K4**), so that the drying chamber was lower than the stokehole.

In some cases, a covering for the stone sides of the drying chamber was found: those at Great Casterton were partly covered with clay (**K4**), and kiln 1 at Stamford had up to two layers of plaster on part of the side (**K1**).

Various other materials have been used in the construction of kilns. The sides of the drying chamber of the kiln at Fishergate in Nottingham (**K15**) consisted of wattling set in sand and covered with clay, while at Wallingford Castle the kilns were built of clay (**K55**). Clay was also used for the sides of the flue at Buckden (**K26**), and in the Ballycatteen kiln (**K31**) to place between the upright stones and to seal the original slate roofing of the flue. Other kilns were probably built of turf. In the possible kiln at Doarlish Cashen, turf has been suggested as an original covering to the fragmentary stonework that survives (**K32**).

Construction of superstructure and drying floors
It has already been stated and shown that the medieval kilns are very similar to the post-medieval ones about which considerably more is known regarding the superstructures and drying floors (see pages 13-14). This similarity plays an important part when suggesting how commodities were dried in the post-Roman and medieval drying kilns.

Types I and II consist of kilns which would have had either a movable kiln hair above the drying chamber (see page 30), or a large drying floor from one wall of the surrounding building to the other. In both cases, the fire was in the flue, and protection was provided for the drying floor or kiln hair. For example, a baffle stone was found *in situ* in Stamford kiln 4 (Figure 26; **K6**), and possible baffle stones, now displaced, were found in the kiln at Faxton (**K10**) and in Stamford kiln 1 (**K1**); an arched flue was found in the Montgomery Castle kiln (**K5**). Similar methods of protecting the drying floors have been found in other kilns. In the Roman kiln 2 at Thundersbarrow Hill (Curwen 1933), the flue was flagged over almost to the far side of the drying chamber, but this may be due to the arrangement of the drying floors, peculiar to the Roman kilns (Figure 4; Goodchild 1943). In the late eighteenth- or early nineteenth-century kiln at Well in North Yorkshire (Gilyard-Beer 1951), the flue was also covered until it entered the middle of the floor of the drying chamber via a vertical shaft (Figure 5). Finally, in the mid-nineteenth-century corn drying kiln that once stood beside the King's Mill in Stamford, the flue is also arched over until it reaches the middle of the floor of the drying chamber (L. Tebbutt pers. comm.). In the kilns of Types I and II, the heat then rose in the drying chamber – fanned out by the battered sides – and through the drying floor or kiln hair above. In each kiln, the sides batter out at about 30° to the vertical.

Large wall-to-wall drying floors can be seen above the drying chambers of several similar kilns; in the old malt kiln at Basingstoke (S.A. Moorhouse, pers. comm.); in the early nineteenth-century corn drying kiln at Tangy Mill, Kintyre (Royal Commission on the Ancient and Historical Monuments of Scotland 1971); and in the mid-nineteenth-century corn drying kiln that once stood beside the King's Mill in Stamford (L. Tebbutt, pers. comm.; Figures 6-7). Evidence of buildings around some of the medieval kilns has been found: at Stamford kiln 1 (**K1**), for instance, part of the superstructure – in the form of roofing slates and stone rubble – was found in the fill of the kiln. The angle of the batter of the drying chamber sides of Stamford kiln 3 (**K3**) seems to suggest that these sides originally existed right up to the walls of the surrounding building (Figure 20). A conjectural construction for this kiln has been put together from all this evidence combined (Figure 21). The size of the drying floor may thus have been 3.96 m east-west by 3.50 m north-south, covering a total area of 13.86 square metres. The Barrow kiln may have had a similar drying floor, 3.36 m east-west by 3.20 m north-south (**K7**). The precise construction of the large drying floors is not known; floors of pierced tiles were introduced in the 18th century (as seen at the mid-nineteenth century kiln at the King's Mill, Stamford: Figures 11-13), but prior to this they may have been similar to the smaller movable floors of the malting kilns.

Figure 11 - Mid-nineteenth century drying kiln next to the King's Mill, Stamford, during demolition. Taken from above to show detail of the drying floor (pierced tiles on top of the rafters). Reproduced by kind permission of the *Rutland & Stamford Mercury*.

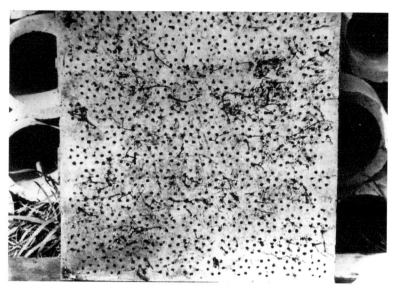

Figure 12 - Top of pierced tile, one of the many used for the drying floor of the mid-nineteenth century corn drying kiln at the King's Mill, Stamford. Reproduced by kind permission of the *Rutland & Stamford Mercury*.

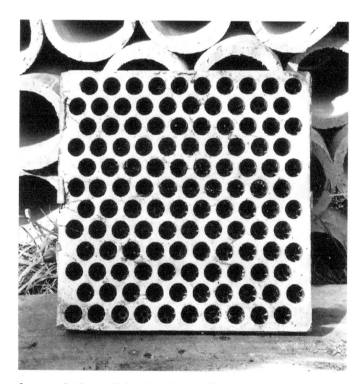

Figure 13 - Underside of pierced tile used for the drying floor of the mid-nineteenth century corn drying kiln at the King's Mill, Stamford. Reproduced by kind permission of the *Rutland & Stamford Mercury*.

These movable floors consisted of either wooden joists on which straw was spread in tightly packed bundles, or a finely woven cloth of horse-hair, presumably stretched across a wooden frame (Barley in Corder 1961; Steer 1969; Brunskill 1970). These hair cloths permitted the heat to penetrate but prevented the grain from falling on to the fire below. The following references show that kiln hairs were used in malting kilns: in a York inventory of 1410 occurs the reference: '*de j cilicio* [kiln hair] *pro hustrina* [malt kiln] *cum ij furgones* [forks]'; and, in 1438: 'sche gat hir an hayr of a kylne swech as men dryen on malt' (Kuhn and Reidy 1969: 'kiln'). The following passage from the *York Memorandum Book* (quoted by Steer 1969) refers to the manufacture of these hair cloths in York in 1487:

A petition was presented to the mayor and corporation asking, among other things, that 'every roper and haster commyng to this citie; and woll set up as a master within the same citie in making ropes, kiln hares, teilds or eny othre thing, pertenyng or belonging to the said craft of ropers and haysters [haysters = hairsters, workers of horsehair] shal pay at his first setting up xiij^s iiij^d.'

Many references to hair cloths occur in inventories as 'haire', 'hayre', 'hayer', 'hayr' or 'here'. One of the earliest references known to me is from 1388: 'Peter del Hill owes 2s for a kiln haire' (Kuhn and Reidy 1969: 'kilne', quoting from *Calendar of Inquisitions Miscellaneous*). Although they were mainly for malting, there is no reason why they should not have been used for many drying kilns, irrespective of function. Many hair cloths occur in inventories of monasteries at the time of the Dissolution: for instance, a 'here for the kill' is recorded in the brewhouse and bakehouse at the Priory of St Thomas near Stafford in 1538 (Walcott 1871). References such as these increase with the vast numbers of household inventories of the 16th, 17th and 18th centuries (Steer 1969).

In the west side of the kiln at Great Casterton (**K4**), opposite the flue, two holes or ledges were found with signs of burning on them: these may have been sockets for the wooden joists of the drying floor. These movable floors may have existed over the malting kiln at Grafton Regis (**K8**) and over the kiln at Faxton (**K10**). Around Stamford kiln 1 (**K1**) was found a floor surface between the edges of the drying chamber and the surrounding building. This would have been to make it easier for someone to turn the commodity when the drying floor was being used.

Permanent and movable drying floors of the types discussed above may have existed over kilns of other types. One does not know what height the drying chambers of the Type III kilns at Sandal Castle (**K13**) and Doncaster (**K14**) originally were. Relatively small kilns of this type may have had a movable floor, but permanent floors in similar structures are known. One was found above a post-medieval malting kiln in Weem, Perthshire (Hurst 1967a). The kiln consisted of a circular funnel-shaped structure, built of drystone walling, 4.83 m in diameter at the top, 3.00 m in height, and narrowing to less than 0.61 m at the base. A flue entered the base of this drying chamber. Access to the drying floor, supported on wooden beams, was by a doorway in one of the surrounding walls at the drying floor level. However, the Kirkstall Abbey malting kiln of Type V (**K29**), and possibly the South Witham kilns of Type IV (**K19**), may have had movable drying floors.

It is impossible to suggest what sort of heat and smoke outlet existed above these drying floors. Modern oast-houses have pivoted wooden cowls to assist the natural draught bringing hot air from the fire through the drying floor, and this was the case at the early nineteenth-century Tangy Mill kiln in Kintyre (Royal Commission on the Ancient and Historical Monuments of Scotland 1971).

One type of drying kiln was ubiquitous in the north and west in the post-medieval period; it had a circular drying chamber with battered or vertical sides, built into the side of a bank or stone platform, with a long flue entering at its base. The fire was at the mouth of the flue, and the hot air travelled along the flagstone-covered flue to the drying chamber, where it rose through the drying floor. From the many descriptions of these kilns, it can be seen that various sorts of drying floor were used. An early nineteenth-century Irish example of such a kiln has been described and sketched by H.T. Knox (Figure 14; Knox 1907).

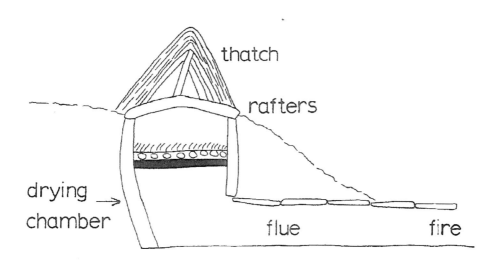

straw

short sticks, transverse to rafters

rafters

Figure 14 - Drawing of a typical kiln in Co. Mayo (after Knox 1907).

Halfway down the drying chamber, bundles of straw were placed over the wooden kiln rafters, and the corn laid on this. Over the top of the kiln, there was a pyramidal thatched roof, in which there was a little door of wattle covered with straw, for access to the drying floor. Straw or hay ropes were used for hinges. There was an opening in the thatch to let out smoke, but little was created in these kilns (Knox 1907). In some cases a linen or hair-cloth sheet was placed on top of the straw bedding, and the corn placed on top of that (Scott 1951). These linen sheets may be similar to the 'streined canvasses' mentioned above (see page 22). Other kilns of this type were open above the drying floor, some being protected by a surrounding building. Such a kiln, of eighteenth- or nineteenth-century date, was found at the Forester's Lodge, near Druidale, Sulby Glen, on the Isle of Man (Cubbon and Megaw 1969). Around the kiln was a stone platform which had steps up to it, giving complete access to the drying floor (Figure 15). Sometimes the building surrounded the drying chamber, and the flue mouth was at the base of the bank outside the building (Feachem 1957).

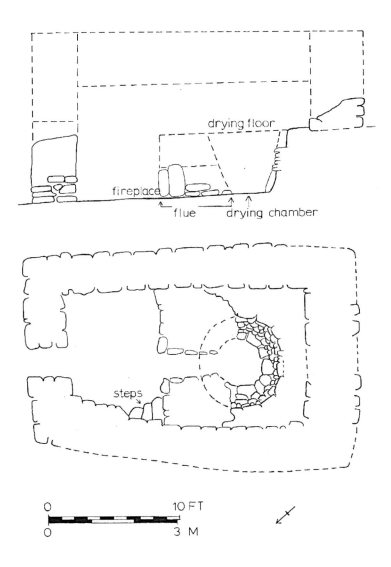

Figure 15 - Forester's Lodge, near Duidale, Sulby Glen, Isle of Man. Plan, section, and conjectural construction of an eighteenth- or nineteenth-century drying kiln in a barn (after Cubbon and Megaw 1969).

Several post-Roman and medieval kilns have been excavated which are similar to the post-medieval examples described above. Some are of Type III, but the majority are of Type IV. However, in some cases the distinction between those with battered sides and those with vertical sides may be misleading. A post-medieval kiln was excavated in Dunipace, Stirlingshire (Dundas 1866): the bottom courses of the drying chamber of this kiln were vertical, but the sides battered out above these. Thus the excavated remains of some kilns may give a misleading impression of the original form of the drying chamber. In some kilns the flagstones over the flue still survive, such as St Blane's (**K25**) and Rue Farm (**K12**), but in the majority of cases they do not. Some of the kilns, such as those at Houndtor (**K18**), were within barns, whereas others such as the Rue Farm kiln (**K12**) may have had only the drying chamber protected. It is suggested that the drying floors of these kilns were similar to the various ones used in the post-medieval kilns of similar form, but this cannot be proved. In the drying chamber of the Rue Farm kiln, small pieces of wood were found which could be the remains of a collapsed drying floor.

The Type III kilns in the caves at Nottingham (**K15**), and those Type V kilns attached to buildings at Jarlshof (**K28**) and Stretham (**K30**), are so similar to some post-medieval kilns that the form of the later kilns may give some indication of the original appearance of the earlier ones. Those at Jarlshof are identical in plan to the kiln associated with the seventeenth-century house on the same site, and also to those used in Shetland until a few years ago (Hamilton 1956). These kilns were also used in the north of Scotland, the Orkneys and the Hebrides as well. They are adjoined to the gable ends of barns, as was the medieval kiln at Stretham, or free-standing nearby. The fireplace is in the outside wall of the kiln, stoked from inside the barn, and the hot air went up a sloping flue (e.g. at Exnaboe, South Shetland: Scott 1951), sometimes from a vertical-backed fireplace. The latter seems to have been the original arrangement of the Stretham kiln (**K30**). The flue entered the bottom of the drying chamber, which in some cases was roughly egg-shaped, and dried the corn on a drying floor set some way above the bottom of the chamber. Above this floor was either a large, barrel-shaped chimney to draw the heat, or a circular-domed roof built either of stone or turf and timber with a vent in the top. The latter is suggested as the original form of the Jarlshof kilns (**K28**; Hamilton 1956). This domed roof construction can be seen over the Nottingham cave kilns (**K11**), which were cut into the solid rock and also had a ledge to support a drying floor. The post-medieval drying floors in such kilns, also supported on a ledge, consisted of a main beam and a number of cross-struts on either side, at right angles to this and resting upon it, which supported a bed of drawn straw or a linen sheet (Scott 1951; Jamieson 1968). The central beam was pulled out in the event of the drying floor catching fire, and the latter fell into the base of the chamber and was extinguished by throwing on handfuls of clay. Access to the drying floors was by a flight of steps from the interior of the barn. The construction of these drying floors may also have been used in several other kilns, such as those of Types III and IV.

Another type of post-medieval kiln, described by Scott (1951: 197–199), may be relevant to the post-Roman and medieval periods. This type occupies the end of a barn, one end of which is divided off by a cross-wall with a gap for the fire. Poles and twigs are laid horizontally from the top of the cross-wall to a beam secured in the end-wall of the barn, and tightly packed bundles of straw are laid on these. Slabs placed on their sides prevent the fire from spreading inwards below the drying floor. Smaller versions of this type of kiln were used in the northern Shetlands, with elaborate baffling to prevent the drying floor catching light. This arrangement of drying floor may have been used in several post-Roman and medieval kilns: for example, that at Highlight (**K33**) and the possible kiln at Doarlish Cashen (**K32**) may have had drying floors like this.

Other methods of drying were used. At Ballycatteen (**K31**), commodities were placed on the flagstones covering the flue, while other kilns such as Letterkeen (**K35**) may have had fires directly below lintel stones on which the corn was dried. Still others were used like ovens, such as the clay-domed structures at Wallingford Castle (**K55**), similar to early Irish kilns made of wattles plastered with clay and used in a similar manner (Evans 1957).

In a lot of cases, the drying floors would have caught alight and needed renewing, especially those where the fire was at the base of the drying chamber, which may have been the case at Altmush (**K39**). In post-medieval times, people drying grain on kilns of this type kept a tub of water close by (Scott 1951: 203). Other kilns, such as at Highlight (**K33**) and Stanhope (**K16**), were built close to streams.

Distribution, dating and origins
Any discussion of the distribution and origins of the various types of drying kiln can only be tentative at this stage. Few Saxon drying kilns have been excavated, and most of those are of the equivalent period in Ireland. Regional and local traditions would have been strong, and many kilns had an individual character, so only broad generalizations can be made. The types defined in this study are

here discussed as a whole, in spite of the broad date range which some cover. One fact, however, is clear: several types of kilns used in post-medieval and fairly recent times existed in the medieval period. Some actually originated in the medieval period: for example, the kilns in barns at Houndtor (**K18**) would not be out of place in many eighteenth- or nineteenth-century settlements in the north of Scotland and the Outer Isles; others had much earlier origins.

The distribution of Types I and II is mainly limited to the English counties of Northamptonshire, Lincolnshire and Rutland (Figure 16). However, this predominantly East Midlands distribution is beginning to change, as one of these kilns was found at Montgomery Castle (**K5**), and one may exist at Fountains Abbey in Yorkshire (**K56**; Figure 43). These kilns do not occur until the 13th century.

The similarity of kilns of these types to the fourth-century kiln at Thundersbarrow Hill has already been noted (see pages 13-14; Figure 4). Several other Roman kilns may originally have been similar to this, such as those at Atworth in Wiltshire (Goodchild, 1943) and West Blatchington in East Sussex (Norris and Burstow 1950). However, the arrangement of the drying floor suggested by Goodchild (1943) differs markedly from the medieval kilns.

During the medieval period there was much overseas trade with the Low Countries, to and from the ports of the Wash (see page 38). Several of the Type I and II kilns occur in the immediate hinterland of the Wash. Perhaps, therefore, the form of these medieval kilns originated from similar drying kilns in the Low Countries – a theory which could only really be tested by a study of medieval drying kilns in that area. In the later medieval period, the idea of square pottery and tile kilns originated from the Low Countries (S.A. Moorhouse pers. comm.). One of the early Type I kilns, Stamford kiln 4 (**K6**), appears to have incorporated the idea of the rectangular drying chamber with the circular one. It is interesting to note that Flemish merchants were trading in Stamford in the early Middle Ages, as they were in other towns of Eastern England (Rogers 1965).

The other types of kilns do not seem to have such a localised distribution as that of Types I and II. Those of Types III and IV occur all over the British Isles, except in the south-eastern counties of England. On the present evidence, the earliest kilns of Type III are dated to the late Saxon period. Those of Type IV are mainly of the 12th or 13th century; but including those at Buckden (**K26**) and Glen Parva (**K27**), this type of kiln probably existed from the early Saxon period. Keyhole-shaped baking or corn drying ovens dated to the 2nd century have been found at Owlesbury, Hampshire (Collis 1968); and one of similar date, containing charcoal and grain, was excavated by Mr W.T. Jones at Old Sleaford, Lincolnshire (M.U. Jones, pers. comm.).

Little can be said in this section about any of the other types of drying kiln. The few kilns of Type V suggest that the drying kiln adjoining a building, and stoked from within, dates back to the 14th century. As yet, no kilns of Type VI, taking into account the post-medieval parallels, have been found outside Ireland. Of Type VII, the kiln at Highlight has possible Roman parallels (**K33**), and that at Altmush (**K39**) is the predecessor of several post-medieval kilns. Kilns in some areas, such as the Isle of Man, which was part of the Norse kingdom from the second half of the 9th century to 1265, need to be studied in relation to their Scandinavian homelands. Several statements have already been made concerning Norse influences on the drying kiln (Gelling 1970; Scott 1951), but this needs to be studied in greater detail, with a knowledge of the drying kilns in Norway.

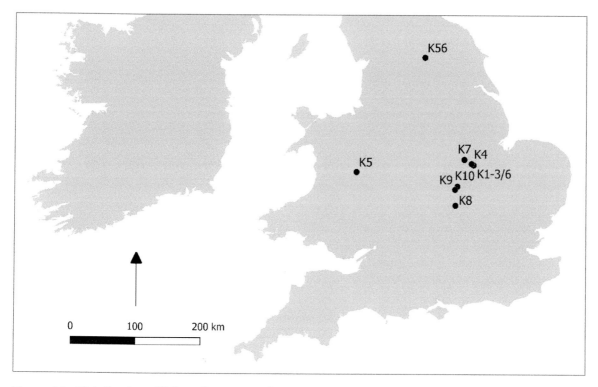

Figure 16 - Distribution of kilns of Types I and II. Great Britain and islands boundary data from Ordnance Survey Open Data © Crown copyright and database right 2017, under the Open Government licence. Isle of Man boundary data from Hijmans *et al.* 2015 under Attribution 3.0 Unported licence (https://creativecommons.org/licenses/by/3.0, viewed 29 June 2021). Island of Ireland boundary data from *Irish Townlands* (https://www.townlands.ie, viewed 29 June 2021) using OpenStreetMap data © OpenStreetMap contributors, under the Open Data Commons Open Database licence (http://opendatacommons.org/licenses/odbl, viewed 29 June 2021).

Historical context

The documentary evidence suggests that drying kilns were much more numerous than the archaeological evidence would allow. There are many references to kilns in early laws, in agricultural calendars, household and monastic inventories, and in contemporary literature. Some refer specifically to corn drying, malting or the drying of some other commodity, but many of the kilns to which these refer were multi-purpose kilns. In this section, the documentary evidence is used with the archaeological evidence to try and put these kilns into their historical context. They occur in towns, villages, raths and farmsteads, moated manor sites, castles, monasteries, and in rural situations not known to be associated with any form of settlement. Owing to lack of space, time and knowledge, a full analysis of the documentary evidence, which is abundant, is not given here.

Drying kilns were held in various forms of ownership, and by various owners, throughout the post-Roman and medieval periods. Different systems of ownership may have occurred in different regions. Some kilns were owned by individuals, or individual families; people of the higher grades of society owned their own kilns. One of the early Irish law tracts, the *Crith Gablach* of the 7th and 8th centuries, which defines the belongings and status of various classes of farmer, states that the *bóaire febsa* should possess a drying kiln (Proudfoot 1961). Welsh legal documents list the buildings which ought to form part of a prince's court, one of which is 'a kiln house for drying grain' (Alcock 1972). Drying kilns were also owned by those who lived in castles: they have been found at Stamford Castle (**K2, K3**), Sandal

Castle (**K13**, **K24**), Wallingford Castle (**K55**) and Montgomery Castle (**K5**). People of lower status also owned kilns. At Faxton (**K10**) a drying kiln was found at the back of a croft owned by 'people of some substance', and they are also found on farmsteads such as at Beere (**K21**), Inishkea North (**K47**), Jarlshof (**K28**) and several others. Other kilns were owned by the church or local ministers, which may have been the case with the kilns at Brixworth (**K9**) and Great Casterton (**K4**). There is a reference of 1550 to a vicar possessing a kiln: 'And he [a vicar] and his successors, shall have a messuage and two barns, and one horse mill, and kilne house, and one acre of land in Spillesby aforesaid' (Whitney 1899: 'kiln').

It is not inconceivable that some individuals owned kilns and charged people who wanted to use them for drying. Kilns would have been owned by maltsters in the towns and elsewhere, and also by monastic and other similar establishments who malted and brewed their own ale.

The Lord of the Manor owned a mill and an oven. In the earlier Middle Ages, the tenants on the manor were compelled to bake their bread in the manorial oven, and to grind their corn in the manorial mill (Bennett 1960; Salzman 1926). These restrictions started to be lifted in some areas in the later 14th century. One wonders whether the Lord also possessed a drying kiln, in which the peasants had to dry their corn before it was ground in the manorial mill. The oven was generally rented to an individual or to the peasants as a body (Bennett 1960), but one cannot say whether a similar situation also existed with regard to the mill.

Some drying kilns were owned communally. The *Crith Gablach* states that the *ócaire*, a man of the free and honourable grade of society, had a share in a kiln, a mill and a barn (Hughes 1972). The Welsh laws state that the ideal complement of a bond settlement of nine houses, closely grouped, included a corn-drying kiln (Glanville Jones 1960). Settlement kilns, probably owned communally, are mentioned in the Laws of Hywel Dda (Richards 1954), which also mention kilns owned by individuals. The early Irish Brehon Laws suggest communal participation in kiln drying (Joyce 1903). Sometimes kilns were owned in common by the people of a township, or its regional equivalents. This may have been the case at Houndtor (**K18**). In Ireland, a mill and kiln were owned by the people of a townland (Joyce 1903).

These many and various documentary references imply that post-Roman and medieval drying kilns were more numerous than the archaeological evidence suggests. This may partly be due to difficulties of recognition, as some of these kilns may have been temporary structures. From the Anglo-Saxon estate management tract known as the *Gerefa* (dated *c.* 1100), information is obtained on the routine of the Anglo-Saxon agricultural year: 'In winter they plough, and in great frost cut timber, prepare their orchards, do many indoor jobs, thresh, cut wood, make a stall for the oxen, sties for the pigs, make a kiln on the threshing floor' (Loyn 1962: 194). This implies that many kilns may have been temporary structures, erected annually, and which therefore do not survive archaeologically in any recognisable form.

In the post-Roman and medieval periods, the consumption of ale was enormous (Joyce 1903; Salzman 1913). Ale was drunk at all times, as the water was not good, and there was a highly organised brewing industry with strict controls over prices and offences. In the towns, there were many inns and taverns which brewed their own ale, in the majority of cases using malt bought from the market. In 1455 it was stated that 'All bruers bought their malt in ye open markets' (Murray 1888: 'malt', quoting from *Rolls of Parliament*, v. 324/2). This suggests that there were professional maltsters in the towns or elsewhere, a suggestion which is supported by the fact that brewers did not want to brew when the price of malt made the trade unprofitable (Salzman 1913). It is possible that several kilns found in towns belonged to maltsters, such as the Stamford kilns 1 and 4 (**K1**, **K6**), some of the Nottingham kilns (**K15**), those at Northampton (**K49**), and possibly that at Doncaster (**K14**).

Malted grain was ground in either a quern or a mill, and either put in sacks or made into cakes and dried. Malt kept for any length of time, either as unground, kiln-dried grain, as meal in sacks, or as dried cakes; and it was often given in payment of rent or tribute (Joyce 1903).

Beer, a new variety of malt liquor, was introduced at the end of the 14th century from Flanders (Salzman 1913). This differed from ale, in that it included hops in the malt and water. It was known on the continent by the late 13th century. Although beer had gained supremacy in England by 1500, the use of hops in brewing was forbidden by Henry VIII, and this ban was not lifted until the last part of Edward VI's reign (Forbes 1954: 140).

The monastic food allowance permitted a gallon of good ale per day per person, often with a second gallon of weak ale (Salzman 1913). Many monasteries were provided with malthouses and brewhouses which had malting kilns, such as at Fountains Abbey (**K56**), Kirkstall Abbey (**K29**) and Grafton Regis (**K8**). There was a malthouse at Nunkeeling Priory in the East Riding of Yorkshire (Gilyard-Beer 1958), and the plan of Tynemouth Priory (Tyne and Wear) shows that there was once a malthouse, kiln house, kiln dodd – the truncated chimney or ventilator of a malt kiln (Wright 1923) – a mill and a brewhouse (Hadcock 1952).

The church had many feasts to commemorate saints, and raised money for church expenses by holding 'church-ales'. These were feasts, for which the churchwardens brewed great quantities of ale from malt supplied by the parishioners and by themselves (Salzman 1926). Some malt may have been bought in a market; some or all of it may have been made locally. The kilns at Brixworth (**K9**) and Great Casterton (**K4**) were just outside the village churchyards, and these may have been owned by the church or the local minister. However, these two kilns may also have been used for the drying of crops brought to the church as tithes.

Following the example of the church, the stewards and bailiffs of the manor instituted 'Scot-ales'. They went round at harvest time and compelled the peasants to give them part of their store of grain to be converted into malt; and when this had been brewed into ale, they compelled the villagers to buy it. However, laws were passed against this practice (Salzman 1926).

An examination of Court Rolls shows that brewing was carried on in every village, which supplied its own needs (Salzman 1913). Thus we can assume either that each village had access to, or owned, a drying kiln, or that the malt was bought in a market. In 1272, the peasants of Martham, Norfolk, drank beer 'brewed on the manor from malt there provided' (Bennett 1960: 184). Brewing was another of the landlord's monopolies, but in some cases a common brewer was known (Coulton 1925). The kiln on the moated manor of Stretham may have been owned by the lord (**K30**).

Private brewing was done by the women of the house, in towns probably with malt bought in the market, but in country farmsteads with malt made either in the domestic oven or in a kiln, if one existed locally. Brewhouses existed in some of the larger houses, and in the castles malting kilns and malthouses were provided. This was the case at Sandal Castle (**K13**), and probably also at Stamford Castle: in the bailey were found two kilns (**K2**, **K3**) and possibly part of a third (not included in the gazetteer, as not enough was excavated). One of their uses was probably malting, but there were probably many others. The site is only a few hundred yards from the King's Mill, where a mill has existed since the 11th century and was included in *Domesday Book*.

Large quantities of corn, malt and ale were exported from King's Lynn in Norfolk from the 13th century and earlier, and both that town and Boston were exporting corn, malt and beer to Iceland and elsewhere from the beginning of the 15th century (Carus-Wilson 1963). Therefore, malting and corn drying were probably undertaken in the hinterland of the Wash ports. Both Stamford (**K1**, **K2**, **K3**, **K6**) and Lincoln (**K48**) are navigable to these ports, and thus the drying kilns in both towns may have contributed to this trade.

Gazetteer of Drying Kilns

Introduction to the Gazetteer

This Gazetteer contains all the post-Roman and medieval drying kilns that were included in the *Archaeological Bibliographies for Great Britain and Ireland* published by the Council for British Archaeology (CBA), from the first edition to that of 1972 (excluding those for 1955 and 1959, which were unobtainable). It also includes other kilns that have come to my notice in following up these references, those which I have come across during my studies, and those which friends have told me about. Finally, it includes unpublished kiln excavations with which I have been associated. The CBA's *Discovery and Excavation in Scotland* reports were also consulted, but contained few kilns specifically dated to the post-Roman and medieval periods. There are many kilns in Scotland which have produced no dating evidence, and many are dated only by relation to settlements or structures nearby. Fieldwork is being done on these kilns, mainly on those of the post-medieval period which survive in a derelict and overgrown condition, but much remains to be done. Therefore, only those Scottish kilns which have been published as medieval have been included.

The corpus has been divided into six basic types, with a miscellaneous section at the end. Sections I to IV are subdivided, to distinguish between (A) kilns within a building, and (B) those which are either free-standing or in which excavation has not been extensive enough to prove or disprove the existence of a surrounding building. These divisions into types were mainly to facilitate the discussion of the possible construction of the superstructures (above, pages 26-27). As there was much scope for experiment in the construction of these kilns, and a variety of kilns and ovens were no doubt used for many purposes including drying, many unique structures have been found, and published as possible corn drying kilns. Some produce evidence which makes their interpretation as a drying kiln quite likely; others cannot be proved either way, and other equally likely interpretations could be offered. These kilns, and possible kilns, are all contained in the miscellaneous section (Type VII).

Following this there is a section containing those kilns about which not enough is known to place them in any of the types. Lastly, there is a section containing three structures published as drying kilns, but which, in my opinion, are better interpreted as having other functions.

In the description of each kiln, information obtained from published reports or from the excavator is presented first. Where I have added my own comments or interpretations, these are placed afterwards, and are separated from the main body of evidence.

Measurements of the total internal length of kilns are from the inner edge of the topmost surviving stone of the drying chamber, to the inner edge of the stokehole, when it is enclosed; and to the end of the walls of the stoking area, when it is not enclosed; and to the end of the walls of the flue, when the stoking area is outside and not defined in any way.

Grid references pertain to the Irish grid reference system (for sites on the island of Ireland) and the British National Grid for all other locations.

Summary of types

Type I

- Built of stone.
- Square, rectangular, or sub-rectangular drying chamber, with three or four sides battering outwards.
- Flue of varying length and width, but not greater in length than the length of the base of the drying chamber.
- Walled stokehole.
- Lower part of kiln constructed below ground surface.
- Date Range: 13th century to late medieval, and into post-medieval period.

Type II

- Built of stone.
- Square or rectangular drying chamber with three or four sides battering outwards.
- Flue of varying length and width; longest flue more or less equal to the length of the base of drying chamber.
- Stoking area not enclosed on all sides.
- Lower part of kiln constructed below ground surface or built in a stone platform.
- Date range: 13th century to late medieval, and into post-medieval period.

Type III

- Generally of 'keyhole' shape.
- Circular or oval drying chamber with battered sides of stone, or wattling coated with clay.
- Flue of varying length and width; longest flue about 2.5 times the length of the base of the drying chamber.
- Stoking area walled or unenclosed.
- Lower part or all of kiln constructed below ground surface or built into a bank.
- Date range: late Saxon to 1600, and into post-medieval period.

Type IV

- Built of stone, or stone and clay.
- Roughly circular drying chamber with vertical sides.
- Flue of varying length and width, flagstone-covered in some cases.
- Stoking area enclosed, or just inside or outside mouth of flue.
- Lower part of kiln constructed below ground surface or built into a bank.
- Date range: early Saxon to 16th century, and into post-medieval period.

Type V

- Built of stone.
- Circular or nearly circular drying chamber, with vertical sides.
- Short, narrow flue, adjoining building or room; stoked from the latter.
- Constructed above ground or within a stone platform.
- Date range: early 14th to 15th century, and into post-medieval period.

Type VI

- Two flues running side by side defined by upright stones.
- Hollow at either end.
- Kiln cut into the ground.
- Date range: *c.* 600 AD up to late 17th century and beyond.

Type VII

- Miscellaneous types which could be drying kilns.
- Date range: late 5th to 16th century.

Type I

This type of kiln is stone built and has a square, rectangular or sub-rectangular drying chamber with three or four of the sites battering outwards. This is connected by a flue in the middle of one of these sides to a walled or partly walled stokehole, either square, rectangular, trapezoidal or oval in shape. They are either contained within buildings, or are apparently free-standing, but in some cases the evidence is not conclusive.

A – within buildings:

- - **K1:** Stamford kiln 1 (Lincolnshire, England)
- - **K2:** Stamford kiln 2 (Lincolnshire, England)
- - **K3:** Stamford kiln 3 (Lincolnshire, England)

B – free-standing, or surrounding building not proved:

- - **K4:** Great Casterton (Rutland, England)
- - **K5:** Montgomery Castle (Powys, Wales)
- - **K6:** Stamford kiln 4 (Lincolnshire, England)

K1: Stamford kiln 1 (Lincolnshire, England)

Coordinates: 503155, 307155

Source: Hurst 1967b; the information below was kindly put at my disposal by Miss C.M. Mahany.

Illustration: Figure 17

Site type: Town

Date: 14th century

Excavated on the High Street, Albert Hall Site A. This kiln, built of local limestone, consisted of an almost square drying chamber, 1.42 m long north-south, by 1.30 m west-east. This had battered sides on the north, west and east sides, sloping outwards at an angle of 35° to the vertical, making the floor of the chamber 1.32 m north-south by 1.14 m west-east. A maximum of four courses survived to a height of 0.15 m. Remains of plaster were found on the floor, and up to two layers on the walls of the drying chamber. Only the lowest courses of the south wall of the drying chamber survived, so it is impossible to say whether it had a vertical or battered side. A flue, 0.58 m wide and 0.23 m long, joined the middle of this side, connecting the drying chamber to the stokehole. The width of the latter varied from 1.10 m to 1.20 m at the south end, and was 0.76 m long north-south. It had vertical sides up to six courses high, 0.64 m, on the west side, and four courses high, 0.38 m, on the east side. On the west side, a further wall has been added, butting onto the south end of the west wall, and on a slightly different alignment. This stokehole extension contained steps into the south-west corner, and the walling on the south and east sides had been robbed. This extension made the total internal length of the kiln 3.36 m, the original length being 2.36 m. The stokehole had a hard plaster floor.

The kiln was higher at the south end and sloped gently downwards to the north end. The floor of the flue had been burnt red, and this burning extended part way into the drying chamber, and few wall stones in either the drying chamber or the stokehole showed signs of burning. A large thick stone was found on the floor of the chamber. This could be a baffle stone, like that of Stamford kiln 4 (**K6**; see Figure 25), which has fallen down. Rubble and stone roofing slates formed part of the fill of the kiln, which had fallen on a layer of dark red burnt clay. Below this there was a burnt, ashy layer containing corn grains and burnt wood fragments.

The kiln was contained in a stone building, with walls of varying thicknesses, 4 m long by 2.90 m wide internally, with a possible entrance in the north corner. A floor surface existed between the kiln and the sides of the building.

The evidence suggests a two-period kiln, in its first phase with a stoking area south of the flue, open on the south side. In the second phase a clay floor was laid in the drying chamber, without fully clearing out the remains of previous dryings. The stokehole was extended and walled round, with steps leading down into it. This may be the reason for the change in alignment of the west wall, as this occurs more or less level with the stokehole extension, in order to provide an entrance in the south-west corner leading to the stokehole steps. Thus the kiln in its first phase may have been of Type II, similar to that at Grafton Regis (**K8**), for example.

Editor's note: This excavation, including Mr Rickett's analysis, has since been published (Mahany *et al.* 1982: 13–28). The 'corn grains' in the fill were identified as wheat and barley; indeterminate seeds, straw and oak charcoal were also identified (Mahany *et al.* 1982: 19).

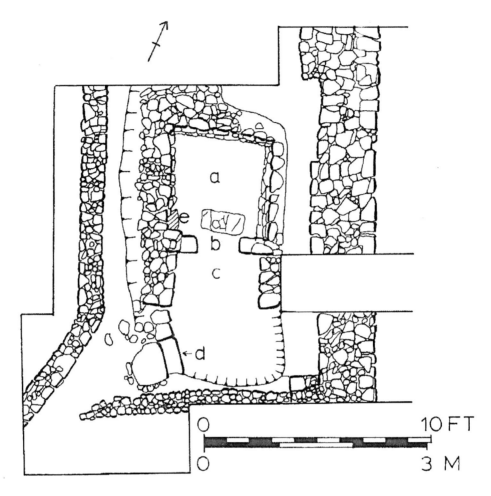

a – drying chamber
b – flue
c – stoke-hole
d – steps
e – plaster

Figure 17 - Stamford kiln 1 (after Miss C.M. Mahany).

44

K2: Stamford kiln 2 (Lincolnshire, England)

Coordinates: 503155, 307155

Source: Cherry 1973; the information below was kindly put at my disposal by Miss C.M. Mahany.

Illustration: Figures 18-19

Site type: Castle bailey

Date: 13th-14th century

Excavated in 1971 at castle site E. This kiln, built of local limestone, had an almost square drying chamber, 1.51 m long north-south by 1.63 m west-east. All four sides battered outwards, at an angle of about 35° to the vertical, making the floor of the chamber 1.14 m north-south by 1.07 m west-east. A maximum of eight courses survived, to a height of 0.76 m. The flue entered the middle of the north side, and was 0.50 m wide, 0.66 m long, and had almost vertical sides surviving to a height of 0.61 m. The stokehole was rectangular, 1.60 m to 1.45 m north-south and 1.22 m wide, with vertical sides surviving to a height of 0.71 m, a maximum of eight courses. It was built slightly to the east of the central axis of the kiln, and had steps in the north-east and north-west corners. The total internal length of the kiln was 4.58 m.

The floor was of a hard, yellowy, mortary material, and sloped towards the south. No signs of burning were found on the floor or sides of the kiln, and one can only assume that this kiln had never been used, or that all evidence of use has been removed by some unknown agency. No grain or other organic remains were found. Rubble was found filling the kiln.

A wall, four courses high, curving towards the north-west corner of the stokehole, may be associated with the kiln, perhaps as part of a fuel store, or it may have been a revetment for the side of a Saxo-Norman quarry which existed to the north of the kiln.

Fragmentary remains of a wall existed to the south of the kiln, and also to the west of the kiln. While the west wall is probably part of a building around the kiln, the south wall was probably in existence before the kiln was built, and has simply been used by the builders to provide a sheltered corner for the kiln. No comparable walls were found on the north or east sides, so one cannot be sure whether the kiln was open or covered by a shelter. It is not even possible to say whether the kiln was ever completed or not.

Editor's note: Excavations at Stamford Castle have since been published (Mahany 1977).

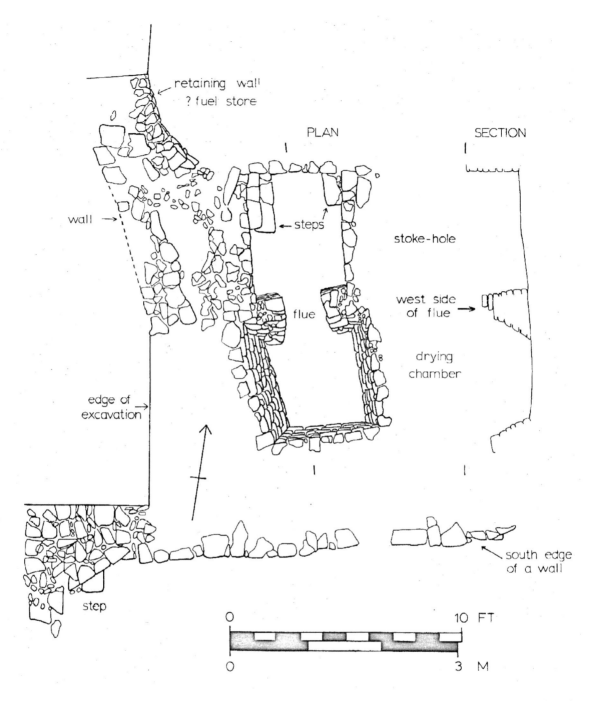

PLAN

SECTION

retaining wall
? fuel store

steps

wall

stoke-hole

west side
of flue

flue

drying
chamber

edge of
excavation

south edge
of a wall

step

| 0 | | | | 10 | FT |

| 0 | | | 3 | M |

Figure 18 - Stamford kiln 2: plan and section from site plans by A.A. Tarwid and R.J. Rickett, under the direction of Miss C.M. Mahany.

Figure 19 - Stamford kiln 2, from west. Scale 6 ft. Photograph by R.J. Rickett.

K3: Stamford kiln 3 (Lincolnshire, England)

Coordinates: 503155, 307155

Source: Cherry 1973; excavated by R.J. Rickett, under the direction of Miss C.M. Mahany, who kindly allowed me to use the information below.

Illustration: Figures 20-24

Site type: Castle bailey

Date: 13th-14th century

Excavated at castle site E. Local limestone, ironstone, and Collyweston slate were used in the building of this kiln. The rectangular drying chamber, 2.34 m long north-south and 2.85 m wide west-east, had asymmetrical, battered, convex sides, surviving to a height of 1.27 m, a maximum of 13 courses high. The lowest courses batter at an angle of about 20° to the vertical, but this increases quite considerably higher up. The floor of the chamber was thus 0.95 m north-south by 0.84 m west-east. Only the north-east corner of the north side of the drying chamber was extant. The flue entered this side, and was 0.61 m wide, 0.51 m long, and its vertical sides survived to a height of 0.41 m. It was only slightly narrower than the width of the base of the drying chamber, and the west side ran continuously with the base of the west side of the drying chamber. The roughly oval stokehole to the north was about 1.52 m north-south and 1.68 m west-east at the topmost surviving course. The west and east sides battered outwards slightly so that the width at the base was 1.22 m. The north side, however, was an angular, concave shape, the top few courses battering inwards towards the centre of the stokehole (see Figure 21, section A-B). This survived to a height of 1.26 m. A flight of four steps had been built into the north-west angle, so that the bottom step did not protrude into the stokehole and reduce the working area. On the east side a square recess had been left, similar to that in the stokehole of Stamford kiln 4 (**K6**; see Figures 24-25). It was backed and lined with stone, and was 0.25 m wide, 0.33 m high and 0.20 m deep (see Figure 21, section E-F). The total internal length of the kiln was 3.96 m.

The floor of the drying chamber was mainly covered with a large Collyweston slate with stones around the edges, and similar materials were used for the floor of the flue. Both the latter and the sides of the flue were extensively burnt, and this bright red and black burning extended part way into the drying chamber. A thick black charcoal and ashy layer, intermingled with bright reddish-grey ash, was found on the floor of the drying chamber and flue. This contained burnt wood, but no corn grains were recognised at the time of excavation. Above this was found a light brown soil with bright creamy-yellow, mortary patches, which extended into the stokehole, and existed a little way up the sides of the kiln. Above this the kiln contained destruction material consisting of rubble and Collyweston slates.

The kiln was contained in a building: part of the south, west and east walls remaining to form a building. This was 3.74 m to 3.96 m wide from east to west, and at least 4.88 m long north-south. There was probably a door in the building, just west of the flight of steps.

Although no evidence was found for a north wall to the building, the natural limestone was cut away to the north of the kiln to form a level platform. Excavation in this area was not extensive, and so slight traces of a wall may not have been detected. In the suggested reconstruction of this kiln (Figure 21), a wall is drawn at the foot of the bank formed by cutting away the natural limestone.

A posthole was found within the west wall, and one within the east wall, of the building. It is possible that these may relate to the superstructure of the building, but the possibility that these are earlier than the kiln building cannot be ruled out. This problem was not fully solved.

Could the square recess in the stokehole, mentioned above, have been for storing tinder for starting the fire in the flue? It is possible that the mortary layer formed above the kiln dust may be the remains of a covering to, or filling in, the stone sides of the kiln, which has subsequently washed into the base of the kiln.

Editor's note: Excavations at Stamford Castle have since been published (Mahany 1977).

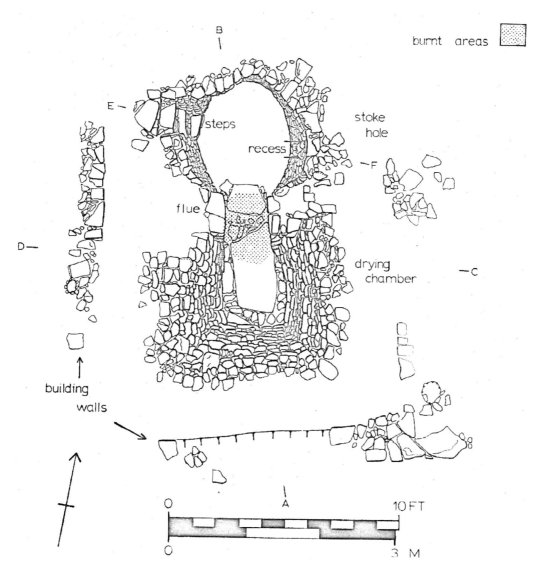

Figure 20 – Stamford kiln 3 (from site plan by R.J. Rickett, under the direction of Miss C.M. Mahany).

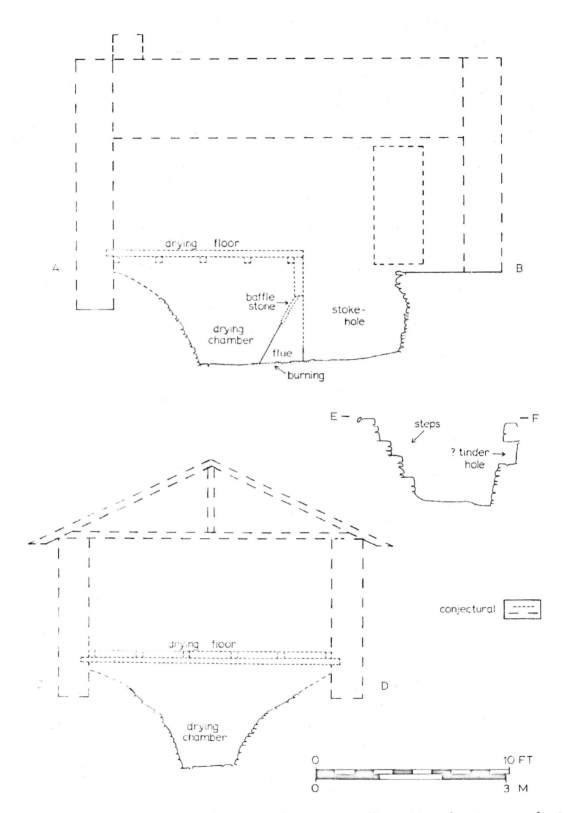

Figure 21 - Stamford kiln 3: sections and conjectural construction (for position of sections, see plan in Figure 20).

Figure 22 - Stamford kiln 3, from north. Scale 6 ft. Photograph by R.J. Rickett.

Figure 23 - Stamford kiln 3, steps into stokehole. Scale 1 ft. Photograph by R.J. Rickett.

Figure 24 - Stamford kiln 3, recess in stokehole wall. Scale 1 ft. Photograph by R.J. Rickett.

K4: Great Casterton (Rutland, England)

Coordinates: 500010, 309100

Source: Corder 1961

Site type: Village

Date: Late medieval or early modern

This kiln was built mainly of local limestone, with occasional ironstone. The almost square drying chamber measured 2.59 m north-south by 2.74 m west-east; the sides were battering out at an angle of about 30° to the vertical, making the floor of the chamber 1.83 m west-east by 1.22 m north-south. This survived to a maximum height of 1.07 m, and the sides originally had a clay surface to provide a smooth fire-proofing, and this had burnt hard where it survived. The natural ironstone floor had remains of limestone flagging in places. The flue entered the middle of the east side and was 0.31 m long and 0.69 m wide. East of this there was a stone-built stokehole with vertical sides surviving to a height of 0.61 m. This was 0.91 m long west-east, and 1.22 m wide north-south. The east wall of the stokehole was formed by a vertical edge in the natural ironstone, and the floor was formed of the natural ironstone and sloped gently from east to west. The total internal length of the kiln was 3.91 m.

The floor of the flue, and a small part of the drying chamber, had been burnt black and red. The burnt grain found in the ashes of the kiln consisted almost entirely of barley, which may suggest that this was a malting kiln (see above, pages 20-21). There was no evidence in the fill of the structure of any form of roofing. In the west wall of the drying chamber two holes or ledges existed, with signs of burning on them, that may have formed sockets for beams. These may have supported the drying floor of the kiln.

The kiln was situated just outside the churchyard wall.

Evidence of covering of the stone walls of the drying chamber here seems to accord with similar evidence form Stamford kilns 1 and 3 (**K1, K3**). The existence of a surrounding building cannot be proved or disproved, as the excavation did not cover a large area.

The only pottery found in the fill was 'medieval or later', and it is suggested, from its similarity to the Barrow kiln (**K7**), which has been ascribed to the late medieval period (perhaps even as late as the 16th or 17th century) that the Great Casterton structure was probably of a similar date. There is no real reason to assign either kiln to so late a date, particularly as it can be seen that similar kilns date back to 13th and 14th centuries.

K5: Montgomery Castle (Powys, Wales)

Coordinates: 322555, 296555

Source: The information below was kindly provided by the excavator, Mr J. Knight, Inspector of Ancient Monuments for Wales.

Site type: Castle bailey

Date: Between the 13th and the mid-16th centuries

This stone-built kiln had a rectangular or square drying chamber with sides battering outwards. It was connected to a square or rectangular stokehole by a narrow flue which was arched over. The floor of the drying chamber was made of tiles. It overlay a thirteenth-century wall and was sealed by a 1540 destruction deposit.

This kiln was originally thought to be a tile kiln. I have not seen the site plans, but the description certainly suggests a drying kiln, as the general plan is very similar to other kilns of this type. The arched flue is interesting, as this is obviously a precaution to protect the drying floor and grain from the fire. A similar device, but in the form of a baffle stone, can be seen *in situ* in Stamford kiln 4 (**K6**).

Editor's note: the Montgomery Castle excavations have since been published, and the report identifies, describes and illustrates several malting and drying kilns and associated features (Knight 1992).

K6: Stamford kiln 4 (Lincolnshire, England)

Coordinates: 503155, 307155

Source: The information below was obtained on a site visit in April 1974 at the kind invitation of the excavator, Mr Garry Till.

Illustration: Figures 25-26

Site type: Town

Date: 13th century

Excavations at 36 High Street. This kiln was built of local limestone, sandstone and Barnack Ragstone. This differed from the rest of the Stamford kilns in that the drying chamber was sub-rectangular, rather than simply rectangular, although it is difficult to get a true impression of the true shape as it was impossible to excavate the top of the sides of chamber. Its sub-rectangular floor measured 1.07 m east-west, 0.91 m wide north-south, and the sides battered outwards at about an angle of 30°, to at least 2.52 m in diameter at the top-most excavated course. At least fourteen courses survived, to a height of 1.07 m. The flue entered the middle of the east side, and was a maximum width of 0.50 m west of the baffle stone, and 0.61 m east of the latter. It was 0.92 m long, and had vertical sides surviving to a height of 0.99 m. The stokehole, to the east of the flue, was roughly trapezoidal, 0.99 m to 1.22 m long west-east by 1.45 m wide north-south. The vertical sides survived to a total height of 1.07 m, and part of the south wall had collapsed into the stokehole. There was a narrow flight of five steps, a maximum of 0.23 m wide, at the east end. In the north side there was a square recess in the wall, 0.17 m wide, 0.18 m high and 0.12 m deep, similar to one in Stamford kiln 3 (**K3**). The total internal length was at least 3.74 m.

The stones and floor of the flue were reddened with heat from the fire, and this extended part way into the drying chamber. Evidence for a relaying of the flue floor was discovered, as this had been continually lowered by the raking out of the ashes. Samples of burnt wood and twigs were obtained from the black ashy deposits in the flue.

This kiln was positioned at the back end of a medieval tenement, away from the street and house, and was aligned west-east, in contrast with all the other Stamford drying kilns which were aligned north-south.

Not enough of the area around this kiln was excavated to prove whether or not it was in a building. However, many Collyweston roof slates and much rubble in the fill of this kiln suggest that there may have been a building around it.

The shape of the drying chamber is something half-way between circular drying chambers with battered sides, such as the late twelfth- or early thirteenth-century kiln at Sandal Castle (see Figure 36; **K13**) and the late medieval kiln at Doncaster (**K14**), and fully rectangular drying chambers of Types I and II. It has been included in this section as it is nearer to the rectangular drying chambered kilns, as one can see by looking at the topmost courses of the sides of the drying chamber.

This kiln is unique in that the baffle stone, for protection of the drying floor and its contents from sparks and flames from the fire in the flue, has been found actually in position (see Figure 26). This has thrown light on the large stone found in the kiln at Faxton (**K10**; see Figure 34), which may have been for the same purpose, but which subsequently became displaced. The large stone found on the floor of the drying chamber of Stamford kiln 1 (**K1**), just in front of the flue, may also be of this nature. The use of some kind of prevention of flames and sparks reaching the drying floor, is also seen in the kiln at

Montgomery Castle (**K5**), but this is the first time that a baffle stone has been discovered *in situ*, and its purpose recognised.

The pottery in the fill of the kiln has been dated by Miss C.M. Mahany to the period around 1250-1300, which suggests a broad date of the 13th century for the use of the kiln.

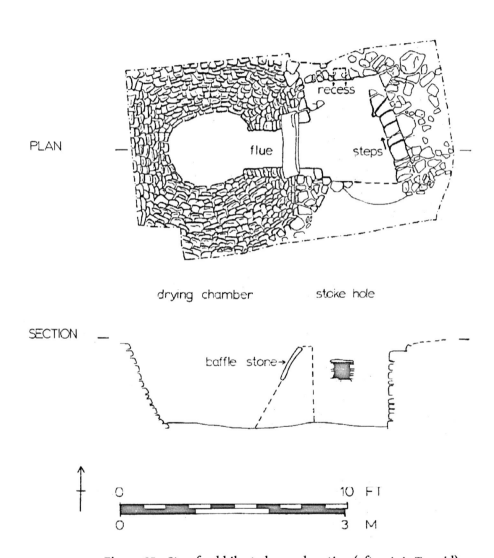

Figure 25 - Stamford kiln 4 plan and section (after A.A. Tarwid).

Figure 26 - Stamford kiln 4 during excavation. Baffle stone *in situ*, stokehole in background. Scale 0.20 m (in 2 cm divisions). Photograph by R.J. Rickett.

Type II

This type of kiln is stone built and has a square or rectangular drying chamber with three or four of the sides battering outwards. This is connected by a flue in the middle of one of these sides to a stoking area of varying size with walls on two sides, but otherwise open. Thus, this differs from Type I only in the fact that the stokehole is not completely enclosed. These occur in buildings, and also free-standing without any evidence of protection.

A – within buildings:

- **K7:** Barrow (Rutland, England)
- **K8:** Grafton Regis (Northamptonshire, England)

B – free-standing, or surrounding building not proved:

- **K9:** Brixworth (Northamptonshire, England)
- **K10:** Faxton (Northamptonshire, England)

K7: Barrow (Rutland, England)

Coordinates: 488960, 315240

Source: Bolton 1960

Illustration: Figure 27

Site type: Rural site

Date: Possibly late medieval

This kiln, of limestone and ironstone, had a 2.21 m square drying chamber, with battered sides sloping outwards at an angle of 30°, and surviving to a height of 1.07 m, fourteen courses. Its rectangular floor measured 1.52 m in length west-east, and 1.37 m in width north-south. Much of the east wall of the drying chamber, which the flue joined, had collapsed. This side had been supported by a wall with a faced east edge of one stone thickness, which butted against the walls of the surrounding building to form a facing to the west end of the stokehole. The total internal length would have been 2.97 m.

The kiln's condition suggested considerable use, the side having been crudely repaired and the original natural ironstone floor lowered some 0.43 m near the flue, presumably by raking out of ash. The floor of the kiln was covered in clean ash to a depth of 0.08 m, suggesting burnt charcoal, and the sides of the kiln showed the typical pink of heated limestone.

The drying chamber and flue occupied the west half of a rectangular stone building, with internal measurements of 6.25 m in length east-west and 3.20 m in width north-south. The eastern half contained the stokehole, which was a roughly sloping hole, slightly more than 0.31 m deeper than the kiln floor and tapering down to an irregular bottom, roughly 1.83 m west-east by 1.22 m north-south. It was partly covered by rough timbers, including an oak beam with several holes lying east-west. Above this was a refuse dump with eighteenth- to nineteenth-century material.

The excavator states that the kiln was not required to produce a high temperature due to its position relative to the prevailing wind, and on analogy with the Great Casterton kiln (**K4**), which was interpreted as a malting kiln, it was suggested that this, too, was of similar function. Comparing this kiln with others of Types I and II, it is certainly a drying kiln of some kind, but it cannot be proved that it is specifically a malting kiln.

'The fact that it was not bonded into the side walls, is the main evidence for concluding that the kiln was no part of the original plan' (Bolton 1960: 130). This does not necessarily have to be the case; it just means that the kiln was built after the construction of the surrounding building, but how long after cannot be determined. The construction trenches for the walls produced a few early medieval sherds, dated between the 10th and 12th centuries. Corder and Barley suggest a date in 'the late medieval period, perhaps even as late as the sixteenth or early seventeenth century', in the absence of any direct dating evidence (Corder 1961). There is no reason why this kiln should not be placed in the 13th or 14th centuries, as similar kilns of Types I and II occur within this date range. This would fit better with the dating evidence for the building surrounding the Barrow kiln, and there is no reason why the two structures cannot be more or less contemporary.

The stone facing to the flue did not survive *in situ*, and it is thus impossible to tell for certain whether this was of uniform width right up to the large stokehole, or whether it opened up into a stoking area, similar to that of other kilns of this type.

Figure 27 - Barrow kiln from east (Bolton 1960 Plate XXV A). Photograph by the Stamford Mercury. Reproduced by kind permission of the Society for Medieval Archaeology.

K8: Grafton Regis (Northamptonshire, England)

Coordinates: 475200, 246700

Source: Hurst 1966; the information below was kindly put at my disposal by Miss C.M. Mahany

Illustration: Figures 29-31

Site type: Monastery brewhouse

Date: 13th-14th century

This stone-built kiln had a rectangular drying chamber, 1.22 m long west-east by 1.52 m wide north-south. The north, south and east walls were battered outwards, so that the floor of the chamber was 0.91 m west-east by 0.99 m north-south, and survived to a height of 0.61 m. Remains of a stone floor were found. The flue joined the vertical west wall and was 0.91 m long, 0.69 m wide and had vertical sides. To the west of the flue was a small stoking area 1.14 m wide north-south and only 0.31 m long. The total internal length of the kiln was 2.52 m.

Above the floor of the drying chamber were found a lot of charcoal and ash remains, containing burnt wood and carbonised grains, to a depth of 0.31 m. Analysis of a sample of the carbonised grain identified 15 grains of hulled six-row barley, nine grains of naked barley, and two grains of oats (analysis by J.R.B. Arthur).

The kiln occupied the south-east corner of the brewhouse and bakehouse, with a large, circular emplacement for a steeping vat to the north. A large oven opened off the west end and circular stone structures, intensely burnt red and black, occupied the north-west and south-east corners, either side of the oven opening. The northern one had a long, thin flue, and the southern one had a wide opening on one side. Both are interpreted as ovens.

The northernmost structure has been intensely burnt inside, and the long narrow flue would restrict access if it were a baking oven. However, it may be better explained as a vat emplacement for heating a boiling vat, used in the brewing process. One of these structures can be seen in an illustration of a medieval brewer in the German work *Hausbuch der Mendelschen Zwölfbrüderstiftung* (The Housekeeping Book of the Twelve Mendel Brothers), dated *c.* 1425. Here the brewer is depicted stirring a vat, which sits in a vertical-sided stone structure. A fire is burning below the vat and is obviously stoked from the arched opening in the side (Figure 28).

Figure 28 - An illustration of Herttel the medieval German brewer from *Hausbuch der Mendelschen Zwölfbrüderstiftung.* Band 1, Nuremberg 1425–1549. Stadtbibliothek Nürnberg, Amb. 317.2°. Image in the Public Domain; obtained from <https://commons.wikimedia.org/wiki/File:Herttel_Pyrprew,_Mendel_Band_I_(1425),_Seite_20v.jpg> viewed April 2021.

The structures in the Grafton Regis brewhouse, also with vertical sides, may also be of this nature. The possibility of the southernmost structure being an oven cannot be ruled out in spite of this, although a similar structure with a relatively wide opening occurs at Fountains Abbey in the brewhouse, and this would best be interpreted as a heated vat emplacement (**K56**).

The large area of floor in the middle of the brewhouse is probably a malting floor, for the germination of the barley.

The thickness of the burnt deposit of ash, grain and wood on the floor of the drying chamber of the kiln might suggest that the kiln hair had caught alight with its load of grain.

Editor's note: In 2021, the Grafton Regis excavations still do not seem to have been fully published (though see Parker 1982 for a summary account). Consequently, Mr Rickett's report on the kilns has also remained unpublished. It has therefore been included in this book as an Appendix (see page 129), since it includes discussion and references additional to those presented in the main text.

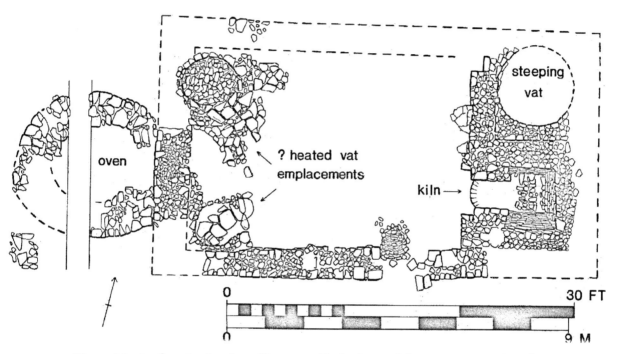

Figure 29 - Grafton Regis, plan of brew- and bake-house (after Miss C.M. Mahany).

Figure 30 - Grafton Regis malting kiln; steeping vat to left (C.M. Mahany). Scale 6 ft.

Figure 31 - Grafton Regis steeping vat emplacement associated with kiln.

K9: Brixworth (Northamptonshire, England)

Coordinates: 474555, 270555

Source: Hurst 1970; excavated by P.J. Woods.

Illustration: Figures 32-33

Site type: Village

Date: Possibly late 13th century

This kiln, of ferruginous sandstone, had a 1.91 m square drying chamber with sides battered out at an angle of between 25° and 35° to the vertical. The floor of the chamber was 1.27 m long north-south by 1.02 m west-east. A narrow flue, 0.48 m long and 0.51 m wide, flanked by single large stones on end, entered the south side of the chamber. The stoking area, faced with vertical stone walls, was a maximum of 0.85 m long north-south, and about 1.12 m wide west-east. The total internal length of the kiln was 2.90 m.

The floor of the flue and a part of the drying chamber had been laid with slabs of limestone which had become discoloured through prolonged burning. A slightly curving channel, 0.24 m to 0.28 m wide, of uncertain purpose, had been cut into the limestone floor of the drying chamber.

It is known from documentary sources that grain was stored in the churchyard in the 13th century (His Majesty's Stationery Office 1910: 600); the kiln stands just south of the present churchyard wall. It is interpreted as a malting kiln.

It is not known whether the excavations proved or disproved the existence of a surrounding building. It is not certain on what evidence the excavator interprets this as a malting kiln, but it seems to be on analogy with the Barrow kiln (**K7**). The latter is described as a malting kiln on analogy with the Great Casterton kiln (**K4**). Thus one can say that both the Barrow and Brixworth kilns are drying kilns, and no more.

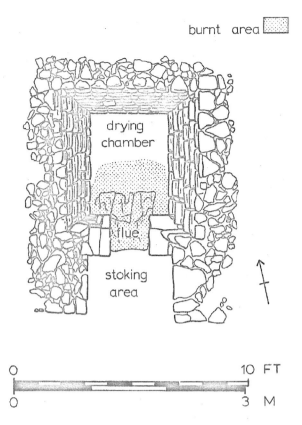

burnt area ▧

drying chamber

flue

stoking area

0   10 FT

0   3 M

Figure 32 - Brixworth, Northants kiln plan (after Mr P.J. Woods).

Figure 33 - Brixworth kiln from south (Hurst 1970 Plate XV B). Photograph by P.J. Woods. Reproduced with permission of the Society for Medieval Archaeology.

K10: Faxton (Northamptonshire, England)

Coordinates: 478300, 275200

Source: Hurst 1967b; the information below was kindly sent by Dr L.A.S. Butler.

Illustration: Figure 34

Site type: Deserted Medieval Village

Date: Mid- to late 14th century

The kiln of local ironstone had a drying chamber 1.37 m long west-east by 0.91 m wide north-south at the top-most surviving courses. The west and east sides survived considerably higher than the other two, the maximum surviving height being 0.99 m. The sides are battered out at an angle of about 25°, and the floor measured 0.94 m west-east by 0.79 m north-south. The flue to the west had vertical sides and was 0.51 m long north-south and 0.61 m wide east-west. The stoking area to the west was a maximum of 0.97 m wide, slightly narrower near the flue, and a maximum of 0.53 m long. There were two wall 'buttresses' to the north and south of the stoking area, which presumably gave strength to this apparently free-standing structure.

In the ash found in the base of the drying chamber, a provisional analysis has revealed the presence of seeds of beans and peas, but no grain was present.

In the filling of the flue a large stone was found, which, by analogy with that found in position in Stamford kiln 4 (**K6**; Figure 25), may have been a baffle stone which has subsequently become displaced. This would have been originally positioned on the drying chamber side of the flue, at the same angle as the battered side, to protect the drying floor or kiln hair with its contents from flames and sparks from the fire in the flue.

Editor's note: The Faxton excavations have since been published (Butler and Gerrard 2021).

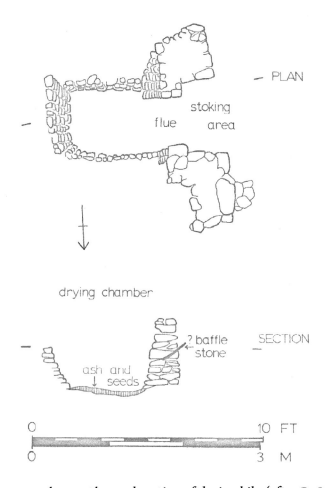

PLAN

stoking
flue   area

drying chamber

SECTION

? baffle
stone

ash and
seeds

0   10 FT
0   3 M

Figure 34 - Faxton, Northants. Plan and section of drying kiln (after Dr L.A.S. Butler).

Type III

This type of kiln has a circular or oval drying chamber, either with battered stone sides, or with wattling coated with clay, to form a basket shape. The flue is of varying length and has vertical sides. In some examples there is a walled stokehole, such as at Doncaster (**K14**); in others, such as Sandal Castle (**K13**), there is only a circular depression in the ground. Some of the other examples do not seem to have had an enclosed stokehole at all, but merely a stoking area behind the flue. Thus, the general impression is that of a 'keyhole' shaped structure. Examples of this type occur in buildings, in caves at Nottingham (**K11**), and as freestanding structures.

A – within buildings or caves:

- **K11:** Nottingham Caves (Nottinghamshire, England)
- **K12:** Rue Farm (Dumfries, Scotland)
- **K13:** Sandal Castle (West Yorkshire, England)

B – free-standing, or surrounding building not proved:

- **K14:** Doncaster (South Yorkshire, England)
- **K15:** Nottingham (Nottinghamshire, England)
- **K16:** Stanhope (Co. Durham, England)

K11: Nottingham Caves (Nottinghamshire, England)

Coordinates: 457433, 339690

Source: Cherry 1972; the information below was kindly supplied by Mr. A.G. MacCormick, Keeper of Antiquities in Nottingham Museum.

Site type: Town

Date: Late 13th to late 16th century

A total of six kilns have been excavated in the caves. These drying kilns have a round or elliptical drying chamber, with sides battering outwards from a flat bottom, with a small narrow flue. This enters the base of the drying chamber, and thus has a roof which protects the drying floor from sparks and flames. There is a stoking area behind the flue. There is usually a stone ledge or 'thrall' around the lip of the drying chamber, upon which rests the drying floor. A beehive-shaped roof exists over the drying chamber, and the whole structure is cut in the solid rock. These drying kilns are entered down a rock-cut stair.

Two of the cave kilns had remains of clay mortared ashlar walls in their superstructure. Drury Hill kiln IIIB had a stone-lined stokehole in its second phase, dated to about 1400. The kiln found at South Parade had a drying chamber 3.05 m in diameter, 3.10 m deep, with the flue 1.52 m deep. This may have been constructed about 1300 and filled in about 1650.

No evidence as to their specific function was found, so they can only be described as drying kilns.

Editor's note: MacCormick has since interpreted these and other examples as medieval cave maltings (MacCormick 2001).

K12: Rue Farm (Dumfries, Scotland)

Coordinates: 290865, 580955

Source: Scott-Elliot 1961

Illustration: Figure 35

Site type: Rural site

Date: Possibly 15th to 16th century

This stone-built kiln, dug into a slight bank, had a circular drying chamber at the west end, 1.78 m in diameter. This had battered sides, with a flat bottom 1.22 m in diameter, and survived to a maximum height of 0.91 m. It contained several large stones which may have been a floor. The base of the drying chamber sloped downwards to the tunnel flue at the east, where there was a vertical step of 0.12 m between the edge of the floor and the floor of the flue. A similar step occurred just in front of the hearth, at the end of the tunnel flue. This may have been to prevent sparks and burning fuel reaching the drying chamber. The flue rises upwards towards the drying chamber, being 0.61 m high, about 0.56 m wide, and has dry stone walls of three courses, and is roofed by large flagstones, three of which were *in situ*. At the mouth of the tunnel flue was found the hearth, below and to the east of which was an air duct. This was 0.20 m high, 0.20 m wide, and it was roofed with flagstones and walled for some of its length. This air duct was 3.05 m long, and the tunnel flue 3.20 m long. The total internal length of the kiln was about 7.92 m.

The fire was at the east end of the tunnel flue, and large quantities of black ash were found to the east of this. Grain husks and wood were found on the floor of the drying chamber. A cobbled area was found to the east of the mouth of the air duct, which had been partly destroyed by a later land drain.

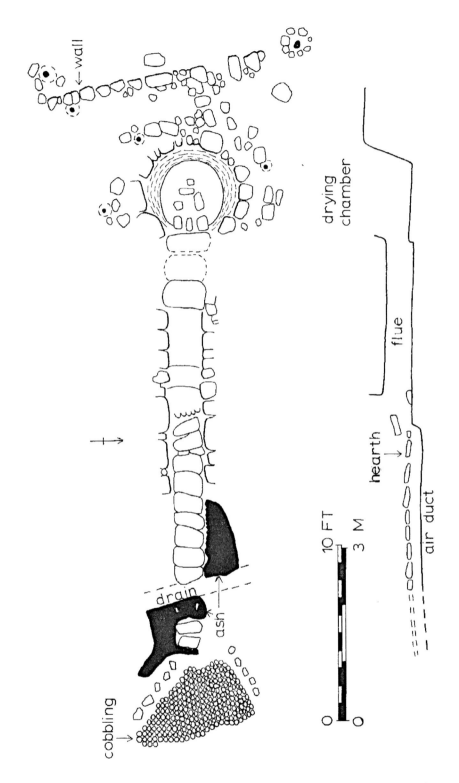

Figure 35 - Rue Farm, Dumfries. Plan and section of drying kiln (after Major-General J. Scott Elliot).

72

The remains of a stone wall were found to the west of the drying chamber, and three postholes were discovered around the latter.

It is difficult to date this kiln precisely. A piece of pottery, dated to the mid-15th century, was found in the wall to the west of the drying chamber, the latter containing eighteenth- to nineteenth-century blue glass in its filling. Mr Truckell, of Dumfries Museum, dates this kiln to the 15th or 16th century, owing to its proximity to Fourmerkland Tower, a sixteenth-century building known to have a fifteenth-century predecessor.

There was some uncertainty as to whether the stones on the floor of the drying chamber were purposely placed or not, and it may therefore be that these are stones which have fallen in after the kiln went into disuse.

The postholes around the drying chamber may be associated with some form of superstructure above it, and the pieces of wood found in the chamber may have been part of the drying floor.

The length of the flue suggests that a fuel such as straw, furze or brushwood was used, as these produce a lot of sparks, and protection of the drying floor and the grain upon it is therefore essential. This can be achieved by the use of a long flue (Scott 1951: 203). In this case, an air duct is provided to supply a draught which would carry the hot air from the hearth up the flue to the drying chamber.

Although a wall was found to the west of the kiln, it does not prove that the whole structure was in a barn, as Mr Truckell suggests. It may be that just the drying chamber and a little of the flue were actually within a building, and hearth and air duct were outside. This arrangement can be seen in corn drying kilns which have been built into banks, such as the post-medieval kiln at Craignavar in Perthshire (Feachem 1957), and other examples of similar date in Scotland.

K13: Sandal Castle (West Yorkshire, England)

Coordinates: 433720, 418160

Source: Mayes 1964

Illustration: Figure 36

Site type: Castle brewhouse

Date: Late 12th or early 13th century

Half of the kiln was cut away by a later kitchen drain, dated to 1317, so only the eastern half remains. It was stone-built, consisting of an oval drying chamber, originally 1.83 m in diameter at the topmost surviving course, the sides battering outwards, eight courses high. The flue entered the north side, and was 1.52 m long with vertical sides, and about 0.76 m high. The stokehole probably originally formed a sub-rectangular depression in the ground about 2.59 m long north-south. The total internal length was 6.45 m. Carbonised grain was found in the kiln, and it is interpreted as a malting kiln.

Editor's note: Excavations at Sandal Castle have since been published (Mayes *et al.* 1983).

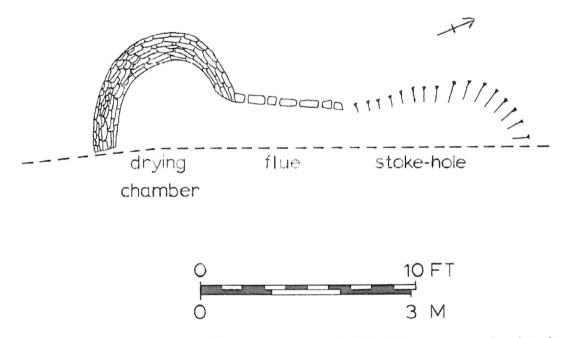

Figure 36 - Sandal Castle brewhouse (after Mr P. Mayes). Half of this kiln was cut away by a later kitchen drain.

K14: Doncaster (South Yorkshire, England)

Coordinates: 457555, 402555

Source: Selkirk and Selkirk 1972a

Illustration: Figure 37

Site type: Town

Date: Late medieval

This was a stone-built kiln with a circular drying chamber with sides battering outwards. A short, straight, narrow flue with vertical sides led into a vertical-sided stokehole with steps in one corner. The stokehole was much narrower near the flue, and the walls gradually got further apart, thus increasing the width away from the flue. This produced the typical 'keyhole' shape.

The description above is from the published photograph. Further information was requested from the excavator but was not received. It has been interpreted as a malting kiln, although I do not know on what evidence this interpretation is based.

Figure 37 - Doncaster kiln: photograph by M.J. Dolby, published in *Current Archaeology* Vol. III, No. 10 (July 1972): 277. Reproduced by kind permission of *Current Archaeology*.

K15: Nottingham (Nottinghamshire, England)

Coordinates: 457433, 339690

Source: Cherry 1972; Cherry 1973; the information below was kindly supplied by Mr C.S.B. Young.

Site type: Town

Date: Late Saxon or Saxo-Norman to late 13th century

North-east corner and south-east corner of pre-Conquest *burh*. A total of eight kilns have been excavated. They were of 'keyhole' shape, varying in size from about 1.83 m by 0.91 m overall, to about 4.88 m by 2.44 m. In general the later ones are larger, but this is not always the case. In Barkergate and Fishergate, six drying kilns were excavated, originally dug into the surface deposits or into the Bunter Sandstone, and had circular or elliptical drying chambers with slightly battered sides, and had single narrow rectangular flues and stokeholes combined. Traces of any superstructure were absent.

One was excavated at Fishergate in 1974; the drying chamber had wattling packed in clean sand around the circumference, over which was plastered clay, which had been burnt red. The burning on the floor extended from the flue part way into the drying chamber. Groups of three postholes either side of the entrance to the flue may have been supports for some kind of an arch or protection for the drying floor. This kiln contained over a bushel of grain and was dated to the late 13th century.

There was a lack of evidence to prove that they were all grain dryers. Some were corn drying kilns, one or two may be malting kilns, but otherwise they can only be described as drying kilns. It cannot as yet be said whether or not these kilns were surrounded by structures of any description, as every site has multi-period timber structures.

Editor's note: In 2021, these excavations have not been fully published, but the *Origins of Nottingham* project has digitised the original site records from many of the excavations, including drawings of various ovens/kilns (Trent and Peak Archaeology 2015).

K16: Stanhope (Co. Durham, England)

Coordinates: 398950, 539390

Source: Hildyard and Snowdon 1955; on Ordnance Survey cards at Durham University, Antiquity No. NY 93 NE 51. The information below was kindly given to me by Mr Robert Young.

Site type: Rural site

Date: Post-14th century

'A circular building on the right side of Allerton Burn about 300 yards north of the back entrance to Stanhope Hall in Allerton Woods. It was almost filled with leaves, earth and fallen stones. The last 1 ft (0.31 m) to 1 ft 6 in (0.51 m) of the interior were covered by a compact mass of fallen flagstones in a thick layer of black ash and grey burnt clay' (R. Young, pers. comm.).

The building was horseshoe-shaped and built into a steep bank above the burn. Near the water the walls remained to a maximum height of 0.69 m, but on the bank side, at the south, survived to a maximum of 2.59 m, fourteen courses. No mortar was used, the stone being set in the clay of the bank and splayed outwards for greater security. This made the maximum internal diameter at the floor level 2.13 m, battering outwards to 3.81 m. The opening opposite the burn was 1.68 m across, closed by a weak wall 0.38 m broad, of which only two or three courses remained. It was still in good condition.

The report is rather ambiguous. The 'circular building' can only be referring to the kiln itself, and it appears that there was no functional flue ('the opening was closed by a weak wall'). However, an opening probably existed there originally, to serve as flue and stoking area.

It cannot be said with certainty whether it is a drying kiln or some other type of kiln. The excavators interpreted it as a corn drying kiln, but many lime kilns, also built into sides of banks to facilitate charging, are also of this type. Some nineteenth-century kilns, originally built as corn-drying kilns, have been used subsequently as lime-burning kilns (Fairhurst 1969).

The date is based on the discovery of a piece of pottery 'almost under one of the lowest courses on the west side', which was of 'unmistakable medieval character', and was suggested to be of fourteenth-century date. The dating evidence was therefore scanty, and the fact that it was still in good condition may suggest that the kiln is of post-medieval date. Certainly many post-medieval and modern 'horseshoe-shaped' kilns have been found in the north.

Type IV

This type of kiln consists of a circular, or almost circular, vertical-sided drying chambers with vertical-sided flues of varying lengths and widths. Some of the flues are found roofed with flagstones, others are not, but this may be due mainly to accidents of survival. The only difference from Type III is that the sides of the drying chamber are not battered.

In most of the examples, the stokehole is not defined, the flue being long enough to partly serve as a stokehole, but mostly the stoking area is outside the end of the flue. The two exceptions to this are Alcester (**K17**) and Sandal Castle (**K24**), the stokeholes of which are defined by stonework.

Examples occur free-standing or within buildings. Kilns in sections A and B are stone built; those in section C are either of stone and clay, or no evidence survives as to the material used.

A – within buildings:

- **K17:** Alcester (Warwickshire, England)
- **K18:** Houndtor (Devon, England)
- **K19:** South Witham (Lincolnshire, England)

B – free-standing, or surrounding building not proved:

- **K20:** Ballymacash (Co. Antrim, Northern Ireland)
- **K21:** Beere (Devon, England)
- **K22:** Glenvoidean (Bute, Scotland)
- **K23:** Rathbeg (Co. Antrim, Northern Ireland)
- **K24:** Sandal Castle (West Yorkshire, England)
- **K25:** St Blane's (Bute, Scotland)

C – The walls of these kilns have not survived, except Buckden (**K26**), which has clay walls to the flue. In plan they resemble kilns of Type IV, but one cannot say whether they originally had battered or vertical walls to the drying chambers. It is only on analogy with other drying kilns that it is suggested that these, too, are drying kilns, rather than ovens.

- **K26:** Buckden (Cambridgeshire, England)
- **K27:** Glen Parva (Leicestershire, England)

K17: Alcester (Warwickshire, England)

Coordinates: 408555, 257555

Source: Hurst 1966; the information below was kindly put at my disposal by Miss C.M. Mahany.

Illustration: Figure 38

Site type: Village

Date: 12th-13th century

This stone-built kiln had a roughly circular drying chamber, 0.84 m in diameter, a maximum of three courses surviving. The flue to the east was about 1.83 m long and 0.53 m wide. Much of the wall of the south side had been robbed. Remains of a roughly circular stokehole, about 1.07 m in diameter, were found, to the east of which was a cobbled area. The drying chamber and flue had been rebuilt, the remains of the earlier kiln surviving beneath the floor of the later one. Thus the total internal length of the later kiln was 3.36 m.

Charcoal and signs of burning existed in the flue, the positioning of which suggested that the fire was towards the east end of the flue. Signs of gentle heating were found on the stones of the drying chamber. Two upturned medieval pots were discovered in a layer of clay at the east end of the flue, where it adjoins the stokehole.

Timber slots, 5.79 m apart, running parallel with the axis of the kiln, and equidistant from it, may have been associated with a building surrounding and covering it (not marked in Figure 38).

Editor's note: These excavations have since been published (Mahany 1994). Gouldwell (in Cracknell and Mahany 1994: 217) examined five environmental samples associated with the kiln, and identified unspecified quantities of coal, charcoal of oak and poplar/willow, and wheat, oats, fat hen, bird's foot trefoil, and common vetch seeds.

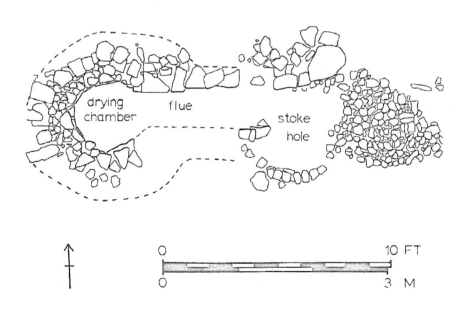

Figure 38 - Alcester kiln plan (after Miss C.M. Mahany).

K18: Houndtor (Devon, England)

Coordinates: 274500, 89000

Source: Hurst 1963; Hurst 1964; excavated by Mrs E.M. Minter.

Site type: Deserted medieval village

Date: 13th century

There are three small corn drying barns of stone, each of similar plan. Barn 3 was 7.77 m long by 3.66 m wide internally, with a stone-built platform at the upper end, 2.59 m wide and standing 1.37 m high in places. In this platform two vertical-sided circular kilns, 1.07 m in a diameter, had been constructed with flues on the north-west side, leading into the barn. These were made of granite slabs and roofed over, leading horizontally at floor level into the bottoms of the drying chambers. The flues were filled with ash and charcoal.

Editor's note: These excavations have since been published alongside the results of another Dartmoor excavation – Hutholes – which also revealed a drying kiln (Beresford 1979).

K19: South Witham (Lincolnshire, England)

Coordinates: 492840, 320520

Source: Selkirk and Selkirk 1968b; Hurst 1967b; excavated by P. Mayes.

Site type: Brewhouse of the preceptory of the Knights Templar

Date: 13th century

Two stone-built grain drying kilns were discovered. These had circular drying chambers with vertical sides, and short, narrow flues to the west. Grain was found in both kilns.

A rectangular structure nearby may have been a vat base, and it is therefore suggested that this area may have been a brewery, and from the plan it looks as though these are in a building.

Further information was requested from the excavator but was not received.

K20: Ballymacash (Co. Antrim, Northern Ireland)

Coordinates: 323720, 366290

Source: Jope and Threlfall 1958

Site type: Rath

Date: unknown

This kiln is mentioned in connection with the report on the Beere kilns (**K21**): 'A comparable but rougher structure with a clay oven beside it has recently been excavated in a rath near Lisburn, Co. Antrim, in the north of Ireland' (Jope and Threlfall 1958). So presumably the drying chamber is oval or circular, with vertical sides and a long narrow flue.

Further information was requested from the excavator but was not received.

Editor's note: This excavation has since been published (Jope and Ivens 1998). The report dates the main occupation of the rath to the 11th-12th centuries and perhaps into the 13th. A very small depiction of the drying kiln appears on the published site plan, but no further information about it is provided.

K21: Beere (Devon, England)

Coordinates: 268955, 103155

Source: Jope and Threlfall 1958

Illustration: Figure 39

Site type: Farmstead

Date: Late 12th to early 13th century

A small drystone-built kiln was found to the north of House I, built into the slope and aligned north-south. It was an asymmetrical structure, with an oval, vertical-sided drying chamber, and a long, narrow flue to the south. The drying chamber was a maximum of 0.91 m in diameter, and the flue was 1.22 m long on the west side and 0.31 m in width. It was straighter and longer on the west side, than on the east side, which curved off towards the east. The kiln survived to a height of 0.51 m, and the total internal length was 2.08 m.

It had a roughly paved stone floor and at the mouth of the flue was found a pile of ash, brushwood and undergrowth. No sign of burning was found in the drying chamber or much of the flue, which suggests that the heat required for drying was not very great.

A second drystone-built kiln was found in the wood to the west, of similar plan to the first, and aligned west-east. This was also asymmetrical, with the flue wall longer and straighter on the north side than on the south. The drying chamber was a maximum of 1.35 m in diameter, the length of the short south side of the flue was 0.76 m, and the width 0.71 m. The total internal length was 2.16 m.

A stone facing existed at the mouth of the kiln, at 90° to the south side of the flue, and part of one existed on the north side. No evidence of any structure was found around the kilns.

Figure 39 - Beere kiln 2 (Jope and Threlfall 1958 Plate XIV C). Photograph by E.M. Jope. Reproduced by kind permission of the Society for Medieval Archaeology.

K22: Glenvoidean (Bute, Scotland)

Coordinates: 199708, 670570

Source: Marshall 1969; Selkirk and Selkirk 1972b

Site type: Rural site

Date: 13th century

This stone-built kiln was constructed in the side of a prehistoric burial cairn, just behind the main chamber. The upright stones on the flue ran back-to-back with the south end stone of the chamber. The roughly circular, vertical-sided, drying chamber was about 1.22 m in diameter. The long narrow flue adjoined the chamber on the west side; it was 1.52 m long and 0.31 m wide. The total internal length of the kiln was 2.95 m.

Evidence of burning and a little spread of seashells were found outside the mouth of the flue. It is suggested that shellfish had been consumed by people using the kiln and was not evidence of the purpose of the kiln itself.

This kiln is similar to many medieval and post-medieval drying kilns in Scotland, which were often built into the sides of banks.

Editor's note: This excavation has since been published (Marshall and Taylor 1977). The report includes a plan of the kiln, and states that 'Residue of burnt grain was recognised lying between the stones in the floor but it disintegrated on touch and could not be examined and identified' (Marshall and Taylor 1977: 19).

K23: Rathbeg (Co. Antrim, Northern Ireland)

Coordinates: 318280, 388050

Source: Warhurst 1969

Site type: Rath

Date: Possibly 13th-14th century

This kiln was found in a position which must have originally been in the inner slope of the bank. The drying chamber was a bowl-shaped hollow 1.52 m in diameter, with walls of boulders set in clay, surviving to a height of about 0.76 m. A straight-sided flue 0.61 m wide led away from the base of the hollow in a south-easterly direction. The mouth of this flue was not excavated. The total length excavated was 2.44 m.

The flue contained a solid mass of charcoal, 0.07 m thick at its neck, which extended halfway across the drying chamber of the kiln. It was here covered by a mass of small boulders, presumably from the collapsed sides of the chamber. The clay along the sides of the kiln had been baked red by the fire.

K24: Sandal Castle (West Yorkshire, England)

Coordinates: 433720, 418160

Source: Excavated by Mr P. Mayes. The information below was kindly given by Mr S.A. Moorhouse.

Site type: Castle moat

Date: 16th century

This stone-built kiln was built over the moat, and was associated with a barn. It consisted of a small circular drying chamber with vertical sides, which was connected to a rectangular, walled stokehole by a long, narrow flue.

Further information was requested from the excavator but was not received.

Editor's note: Excavations at Sandal Castle have since been published (Mayes *et al.* 1983).

K25: St Blane's (Bute, Scotland)

Coordinates: 209491, 653446

Source: Milligan 1963

Site type: Rural site

Date: Post-dating the 12th-13th centuries

This stone-built kiln was found just outside the wall surrounding the monastic settlement, and an old turf field dyke lay across the front of it.

The drying chamber was crudely built; the stones were unfashioned and not in regular courses, and many had fallen out. A low, semi-circular wall around the top of the kiln supported the sides of the drying chamber. The flue was 3.05 m long, 0.61 m wide, and 0.61 m high, and was level up to the drying chamber. Two lintel stones covering the flue remained *in situ*. A stone was laid across the floor of the flue just before it entered the drying chamber. This, the excavator suggests, was to prevent burning embers drifting in.

The flue stones were reddened by heat from the fire, and ash and cinders were found in the flue.

It was not stated whether the walls of the drying chamber were vertical or battered.

K26: Buckden (Cambridgeshire, England)

Coordinates: 519000, 267500

Source: Addyman 1963

Site type: Rural settlement

Date: Early Saxon

This kiln-like structure was found close to a sunken hut. It consists of two curving, parallel lines of red burnt clay about 1.45 m long and 0.18 m deep, forming a channel 0.24 m wide internally, being slightly wider at the south-east end. Within this channel, broken slabs of limestone, burnt on one side only, were found; these seemed to be collapsed roofing. The gravel floor had also been burnt. An oval, shallow depression at the west end of this channel, 1.68 m long west-east by 0.84 m wide north-south, also contained broken limestone slabs burnt on one side. No other indication of heating was found in this pit. The irregularly shaped, almost rectangular pit at the east end, 1.83 m long north-south by 0.99 m west-east, and 0.46 m deep, was filled with dark brown soil and charcoal. The gravel around the sides had been burnt red. The channel or flue joins the pits on the narrower sides.

The deeper pit at the south side has been interpreted as a fire pit and the channel as a flue which conducted heat to the shallow pit where limestone slabs represent the base of an oven or kiln of which the superstructure has gone.

This is either a kiln or an oven of some description. The layout is reminiscent of drying kilns excavated elsewhere. At Peninerine and Griminish in the Outer Hebrides, two post-medieval corn-drying kilns at the end of barns were excavated (Whitaker 1957). The layout of those kilns is very similar to that at Buckden, with curving flues between the drying chamber and fireplace (see Figure 8). The evidence of the position of burning, within the flue and stokehole, and not in the possible drying chamber, is certainly suggestive of a drying kiln, rather than an oven.

K27: Glen Parva (Leicestershire, England)

Coordinates: 457400, 298100

Source: Hurst 1967b; the information below was kindly supplied by Mr K.C. Clarke.

Illustration: Figure 40

Site type: Partially moated shrunken medieval village

Date: Early medieval

This kiln consisted of an almost circular, moderately steep-sloped hollow forming the drying chamber, 1.60 m to 1.75 m in diameter, and 0.43 m deep. To the south-east there was a long, slightly curving flue 2.52 m long and varying from 0.76 m to 0.91 m in width. It had sloping sides steeper than those of the drying chamber. The total length of the kiln was about 4.10 m.

The drying chamber had an almost clean flat floor; that of the flue had intense heat reddening at its neck, which extended a little way into the drying chamber. Behind the burning, in the middle of the flue, were the rakings from the fire, a pile of sooty material overlying much grey ash. Cobbles were laid at the extreme south-east end of the flue. The kiln was cut into the natural subsoil, and the bottom was not of a uniform depth.

In plan, it can be compared with kilns at Rathbeg (**K23**), and Glenvoidean (**K22**). The fire at Glen Parva had obviously been at the neck of the flue, which is the same position as that at Rathbeg. Thus the rest of the long flue, behind the fire, serves as a stoking area.

There was no evidence to suggest its function, but the similarity to other drying kilns, and the fact that the fire is not in the circular hollow, suggest that it is a drying kiln of some description rather than an oven.

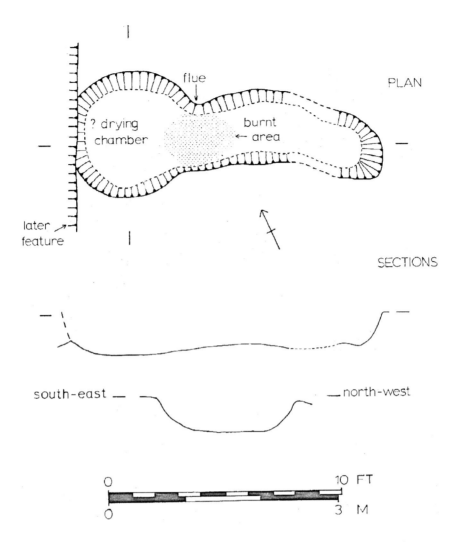

PLAN

flue

? drying chamber

burnt area

later feature

SECTIONS

south-east

north-west

0 — 10 FT
0 — 3 M

Figure 40 - Glen Parva kiln plan and section (after Mr K.C. Clarke).

Type V

This type consists of stone-built kilns with circular, or nearly circular, straight-sided drying chambers and short flues. These are either totally within buildings, and have the flue forming an opening in a wall of a room, or are adjoined to one corner or one end of a building. In the latter case, the drying chamber is almost a separate building in itself, but it is stoked from within the main building.

- **K28:** Jarlshof (Shetland, Scotland)
- **K29:** Kirkstall Abbey (West Yorkshire, England)
- **K30:** Stretham (West Sussex, England)

K28: Jarlshof (Shetland, Scotland)

Coordinates: 439819, 1109551

Source: Hamilton 1956; the information below was kindly sent by Mr J.R.C. Hamilton.

Site type: Farmstead

Date: 14th-15th century

This stone-built kiln adjoined the north-west corner of the building. It had a roughly circular drying chamber, 1.14 m east-west by 1.37 m north-south, with vertical-sided walls 0.38 m to 0.61 m thick. It had a flue, leading in from the corner of the barn on the east side, which was 0.46 m long and 0.61 m wide. The flue and chamber were partly flagged.

The fire was lit at the entrance to the flue, where the stones were reddened and crackled by the heat on both wall faces.

This kiln succeeded an earlier one, the outer arc of which survived to the north-west of the later kiln. It was of similar type, roughly circular, about 1.32 m in diameter, with vertical sided walls 0.31 m thick. The flue probably originally led off from the corner of the barn, similar to the later arrangement.

They are both interpreted as corn drying kilns, from their similarity to later surviving kilns in Shetland, and also to that of the seventeenth-century house of Jarlshof.

K29: Kirkstall Abbey (West Yorkshire, England)

Coordinates: 426000, 436100

Source: Pirie 1966

Site type: Monastery malthouse

Date: 15th century

Adjoining the north-east corner of the malthouse was found a circular stone structure about 1.83 m in diameter, with a short narrow flue to the west. The flue mouth is thus flush with the east wall of the malthouse.

On the plan this is labelled as a kiln, presumably used for the drying of malt.

K30: Stretham (West Sussex, England)

Coordinates: 520105, 113725

Source: Hurst 1965; the information below was kindly sent by Mr A. Barr-Hamilton.

Illustration: Figure 41

Site type: Moated manor

Date: Early to mid-14th century

The drying kiln consisted of an originally circular drying chamber, adjoining the east end of a building, with a flue to the west, in the middle of the end wall of the building. The drying chamber, built of ironstone boulders in clay, resting on a single course of sharp flints in white mortar, was 3.05 m in diameter internally with walls 0.53 m thick. The vertical wall survived to a maximum height of 0.46 m, and the floor of the chamber was of clay. Some ash was found upon it. The flue to the west went 0.71 m into the wall of the building, but was not connected at the surviving level to the drying chamber. The flue had vertical sides of squared blocks of siltstone on the north and south sides, and was 0.38 m in width. The total length of the structure was 4.35 m.

To the west of the flue the clay floor of the building had been burnt red by the raking out of hot ashes from the flue. Several uneven layers of ash and reddened clay existed as if the floor had been re-laid several times.

Only fragmentary remains of the building associated with the kiln survived. It was stone-built, 7.54 m in width internally and at least 14.63 m long internally.

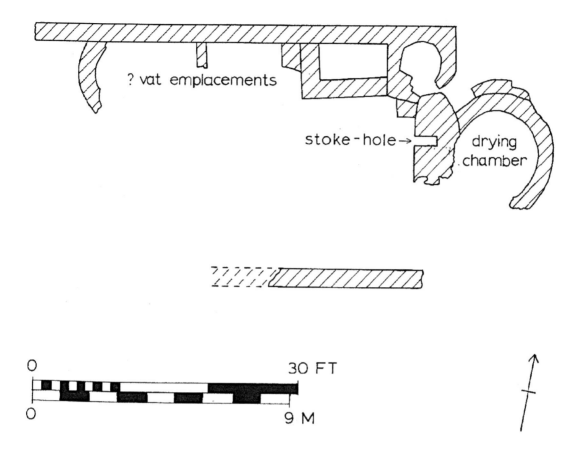

? vat emplacements

stoke - hole →

drying chamber

0   30 FT

0   9 M

Figure 41 - Stretham plan of malthouse and drying kiln (after Mr A. Barr-Hamilton).

The arrangement of flue and drying chamber suggests that the former was connected to the latter through the upper courses of the end wall of the building, which did not survive. This arrangement would be similar to post-medieval drying kilns in Scotland, where the flue is lower at the fireplace next to the barn, and higher where it enters the drying chamber (Jamieson 1968).

Carbonised grains of barley were found, and it is known that a number of acres of barley existed in the manor at the time of the medieval survey. Could this building have been the brewhouse? If so, then a likely explanation for the structures on the north side of the building is that these are emplacements for vats, mash tubs or brewing leads, and the roughly circular structure in the north-west corner, interpreted as an oven, may have been a heated emplacement for a boiler. Similar structures have been found in the brewhouse at Grafton Regis (**K8**). Thus, the kiln would have been used for the malting of barley, which is supported by the grain evidence.

Editor's note: This excavation has since been published (Funnell 2009).

Type VI

This type of kiln consists of two parallel flues running side by side, defined by upright stones with a circular, or roughly circular, hollow at either end.

- **K31:** Ballycatteen (Co. Cork, Ireland)

K31: Ballycatteen (Co. Cork, Ireland)

Coordinates: 158198, 45919

Source: Ó Ríordáin and Hartnett 1944

Illustration: Figure 10

Site type: Rath

Date: between 7th and late 17th century

This kiln was built close to the interior rampart, and no evidence of any surrounding structure was found. It consisted of three parallel lines of stones, set upright, 0.31 m high, forming two flues 0.38 m wide and 2.74 m long. The total width was between 0.91 m and 1.07 m. These flues opened on to a shallow pit at either end. That at the west end was 1.37 m in diameter north-south, and that at the east end was an irregular, rectangular shape, 1.37 m west-east by 1.22 m north-south.

The gaps between the flue stones were sealed with a stiff daub. They were reddened by heat, and the soil beside and below them was a bright red. The filling of the flues contained several dressed slates, and much baked clay. On this evidence it is suggested that the flues were roofed with slates and sealed with clay to make them airtight.

The dating of this kiln is a problem. On the main published plan, it underlies a black layer, dated on slender evidence to the later 6th century and early 7th century AD. However, in the description the kiln was found 'at the edge, and just outside, the black layer' (Ó Ríordáin and Hartnett 1944). The rath was occupied up to the later 17th century, and so it could be that the kiln is of any date between about AD 600 and the later 17th century.

No evidence as to its function was found. The excavator pointed out that it was similar to a nineteenth-century flax drying kiln at Meenanea, Co. Tyrone (Figure 10; Davies 1938). This consisted of a semi-cylindrical wall of dry masonry at one end, about 0.91 m in internal diameter, and 1.83 m high. From its ends there ran out a flue at ground level, about 3.05 m long and 0.46 m high. This was built of upright stones on both sides and was divided down the centre also by a line of stones. This was covered with large slabs. The fire was lit in the semi-circular stone structure at the end, when the wind was in a suitable direction to cause the hot air to pass below the slabs covering the flue. The flax was laid out on these and slowly dried.

However, this does not mean that the Ballycatteen kiln was necessarily used for flax drying. It is not stated in the report whether either of the hollows at the ends of the flue showed any signs of burning. The evidence available does, however, suggest that this could be a drying kiln of some description.

Type VII

This section contains miscellaneous structures which may or may not be drying kilns. Some are certainly drying kilns, including some which cannot be paralleled in other known structures of any period, and some which may have been partly destroyed, giving a misleading impression of the original form. Others are published as possible corn drying kilns, for want of any better interpretation, but with no positive evidence. However, it must be remembered that, while they may have been drying kilns for various commodities, other explanations may be equally valid.

The first section contains those kilns which are basically of square or rectangular form, and the second section those which are basically of oval or circular form.

A – basically square or rectangular:

- **K32:** Doarlish Cashen (Isle of Man)
- **K33:** Highlight (Glamorgan, Wales)
- **K34:** Hullasey (Gloucestershire, England)
- **K35:** Letterkeen (Co. Mayo, Ireland)
- **K36:** Lundy Island (Devon, England)
- **K37:** Uisneach (Co. Westmeath, Ireland)
- **K38:** Underhoull (Shetland, Scotland)

B – oval, circular or nearly circular:

- **K39:** Altmush (Co. Meath, Ireland)
- **K40:** Garranes (Co. Cork, Ireland)
- **K41:** Michelham Priory (East Sussex, England)
- **K42:** Tintagel (Cornwall, England)
- **K43:** Merthyr Dyfan (Glamorgan, Wales)

K32: Doarlish Cashen (Isle of Man)

Coordinates: 223555, 478155

Source: Gelling 1970

Site type: Farmstead

Date: Anywhere the between the second half of the 9th century and the 13th century

This kiln, possibly constructed of turf, was built into a turf enclosure wall. It consisted of a rectangular drying chamber 3.40 m wide north-west to south-east, by 2.10 m long. In places its edge was defined by a stone footing; elsewhere it was dug slightly into the subsoil. The main flue, which entered the middle of the south-west side of the chamber, consisted of upright slabs on both sides. It was 2.60 m long, 1.30 m wide where it entered the chamber, and narrowed to 0.59 m at the mouth. It had subsidiary flues on the north-west and south-east sides, both entering the end of the chamber at roughly 90°, at the same end as the main flue. The former flue was 0.66 m wide, and the latter 0.50 m wide. A layer of wood and peat ash covered the bottom of the main flue and extended into the subsidiary flues. A slot 0.13 m deep ran across the mouth of the main flue, and it has been suggested that this held a board for closing the flue when necessary. Two stones were found in the centre of the drying chamber; these may have been for a central support. The total length of the kiln was 5.42 m.

It is possible that this is a drying kiln of some kind, the arrangement of the flues suggesting that it was built with due consideration for different wind directions. On the other hand, some other form of structure, such as an animal pen, must not be ruled out.

K33: Highlight (Glamorgan, Wales)

Coordinates: 309755, 169955

Source: Thomas 1967; the information below was kindly sent by Mr H.J. Thomas.

Site type: Deserted medieval village

Date: 12th to 14th century

This kiln consisted of a crudely built drystone channel, 0.38 m wide, 1.83 m long on the west side and 1.45 m long on the east side. The original height is estimated as being between 0.61 m and 0.91 m. A modern drainage ditch cut through part of the south end.

At the north end the sides of the channel showed signs of severe burning and a large patch of charcoal was found on the floor at this end. The remaining part of the channel was unburnt. An associated black layer produced much carbonised grain mixed with burnt straw and brushwood (or small twigs). A quern fragment was found in the kiln.

No evidence of any covering building was found, but only a small area was excavated. The kiln was situated about 6.10 m from a small stream, which may have been deliberate, to enable the fire to be put out in emergencies. Evidence was found of corn drying on this site, previous to the use of this kiln.

A drying chamber may have originally existed at the south end of the channel, and subsequently been destroyed. If, however, the kiln was found more or less in its original form, then the corn would probably have been placed on a drying floor of some kind at the south end, with a fire at the north end producing the heat.

In this form it is similar to a Roman drying kiln found at Lynch Farm, Orton Waterville, Peterborough (Wild 1973), and one at Cwm-Brwyn, Carmarthenshire (Ward 1907). The latter had a stokehole outside a rectangular stone channel, which was enclosed at the opposite end.

K34: Hullasey (Gloucestershire, England)

Coordinates: 397324, 199179

Source: Baddelay 1910

Site type: Deserted medieval village

Date: 14th century

This structure resembles, in section, a big jar. The total depth was 1.98 m, the bottom cut out of the solid rock, and the top formed of drystone walling with vertical edges. The rock-cut part was slightly concave and was wider than the stone-built mouth, which measured 1.52 m by 1.68 m. The external measurement was 2.69 m square. Traces of fire were found at the top, but none below.

1.22 m to the north was another stone structure, connected to the larger one by a channel 0.61 m wide and 1.22 m high. This sloped downwards to the main structure, owing to the differing heights of the two constructions. The smaller structure was built of drystone walling, resembling a horseshoe in shape, with the north side longer than the south. It lay parallel to the larger structure, the ends of the walling terminating abruptly in large upright slabs 0.91 m high, that of the south side set back to allow for the channel entrance. The smaller structure was 1.37 m from the present ground surface, and both this and the connecting channel formed an L-shape adjoining the main structure. Traces of fire in the smaller structure were few. Both structures were later used as rubbish pits.

The interpretation of this structure as a possible corn drying kiln was suggested in the Beere report (Jope and Threlfall 1958). A fire lit at the bottom of the main structure could have dried anything laid across the top, with the smaller structure to aid the draught, but why have something so elaborate? The sides of the rock which formed the lower part of this structure may have been shattered by frost action, thus destroying all evidence of fire. However, the structure may have been something completely different, such as a settling tank, later used to deposit and burn off rubbish.

K35: Letterkeen (Co. Mayo, Ireland)

Coordinates: 98145, 307594

Source: Ó Ríordáin and Macdermott 1952

Site type: Rath

Date: Possibly 7th century

This possible kiln was found in a large area of intensive burning, containing charcoal and red ash (presumably peat), outside a hut. It consisted of a rectangle formed by upright slabs, set in the natural clay to a depth of 0.60 m. This trench measured 1.60 m east-west by 0.51 m north-south. Two lintel stones, over these upright slabs, remained *in situ* at its eastern end.

The filling of the structure contained some charcoal. It is interpreted as a corn drying kiln, in which the corn to be dried was placed on the lintel stones, with a fire burning underneath. A shattered quern was found nearby, which supports the theory that grain was being dried prior to grinding.

This structure may have had several other purposes, as well as the suggested drying of corn. Other commodities could have been dried upon it, or perhaps it may even have been used as an oven with food being cooked inside, after it had been heated.

K36: Lundy Island (Devon, England)

Coordinates: 213350, 145880

Source: Hurst 1965; Hurst 1967b; the information below was kindly sent by Mr K.S. Gardner.

Site type: Farmstead

Date: 13th century

At Widow's Tenement a stone longhouse was excavated. Adjoining the long north side at the west end, which may have been the living end, was a fireplace or possible corn drying kiln. It was roughly square, with the south side completely open to the house.

This is probably an ordinary domestic fireplace, over which cooking and drying took place. It is quite possible that corn was dried over this, as the drying of corn over the domestic hearth is recorded by Boswell in his *Journal of a Tour to the Hebrides* (Whitaker 1957). He records, at Screapadal on the Isle of Raasay, the drying of small quantities of corn in a wattle and clay pot, as and when it was required.

K37: Uisneach (Co. Westmeath, Ireland)

Coordinates: 229572, 248795

Source: Macalister and Praeger 1928

Site type: Rath

Date: *c.* 150 AD, but occupation before and after this

The remains of a stone structure were found in the angle of two of the banks dividing the rath interior. It consisted of a rectangular floor, partly outlined by one course of stones, with two courses in the north-east corner. A long stone-lined entrance led into the south-west corner of one of the longer sides of the structure. The total measurements were 2.03 m by 1.68 m. It was full of ashes and was interpreted as a ruined and rifled cairn chamber, which had subsequently been used as a receptacle for the debris of fires.

Proudfoot has suggested that this was 'possibly an oven or kiln for drying grain' (Proudfoot 1961). However, this may alternatively have served some other function, perhaps for the penning of animals. The presence of ashes alone does not prove this is a drying kiln, as ashes have been used in the preservation of all kinds of food (Scott 1948).

K38: Underhoull (Shetland, Scotland)

Coordinates: 457345, 1204355

Source: Small 1966

Site type: Viking settlement

Date: 9th-10th century

A stone-built structure was found outside the north-east corner of a long house. It consisted of a central rectangular hearth, surrounded by upright stones, measuring 0.91 m north-south by 0.38 m east-west. There were a number of fire-cracked pebbles in this. It was surrounded on all sides by a narrow channel 0.23 m wide, with sides of upright slabs, and in part covered by flat stones. A further channel linked this to the outside north wall of the house. It was suggested that this is a device to give considerable draught at the hearth. The total dimensions are 1.68 m north-south, by 2.13 m east-west. It is interpreted as 'some sort of drying chamber, probably for grain' (Small 1966).

This may well be a kiln or oven of some kind, with many and varied functions. It is surrounded by a building which would once have adjoined the long house. Perhaps it was some kind of curing-house for the smoking of fish, for instance – a practice carried on for many centuries in the Northern Isles (Scott 1948).

K39: Altmush (Co. Meath, Ireland)

Coordinates: 278874, 287922

Source: Moore 1958

Site type: Rural site

Date: Pre-1400, possibly Early Christian or early medieval.

This circular, stone-built kiln was about 0.61 m in diameter at the base, battering out to 1.22 m in diameter at the highest surviving course. It was 1.52 m in depth and had no evidence for a flue, thus resembling a round bowl.

The stones and clay floor of this kiln had been burnt bright red. No evidence for its function was found, but Ó Ríordáin identified it as a corn drying kiln, by analogy with similar structures known to be corn drying kilns.

It is stated in the report that no flue was found, but an outhouse existed where one might expect to find a flue. In spite of this apparent lack of a flue, the existence of one was inferred, because other corn drying kilns have them.

If, however, it is interpreted as having no flue, it would be similar to a post-medieval example found in Skelpick Burn Wood, Sutherland (Horsburgh 1868), said to be a pit for cooking deer, but which Sir Lindsay Scott thinks could be a grain drying kiln (Scott 1951: 201).

K40: Garranes (Co. Cork, Ireland)

Coordinates: 147337, 64003

Source: Ó Ríordáin 1942

Site type: Rath

Date: 5th-6th century

A setting of stones, forming an irregular arc of a circle, the chord of which was about 1.83 m, was found and interpreted as part of the base of a hut. It was only one course high, and no burning was found. Near it was found the lower stone of a quern. In the rath were found crucibles, moulds, metal and glass remains; this suggested the presence of a manufacturing workshop.

Proudfoot suggests that this structure was 'possibly for drying grain although it may have been used for industrial purpose' (Proudfoot 1961).

There is so little evidence to put any interpretation on this structure at all, let alone to call it a grain drying kiln.

K41: Michelham Priory (East Sussex, England)

Coordinates: 555800, 109400

Source: The information below was kindly sent by Mr L. Stevens.

Site type: Priory hall

Date: Possibly 15th-16th century

Two possible drying kilns adjoined the east end of an earlier medieval hall. Both were multi-angular inside and horseshoe-shaped on the outside, and were constructed of sandstone. The larger chamber was about 4.00 m in diameter internally, and the smaller one about 2.40 m. Neither survived much higher than its floor level. The floor of the larger chamber was composed of flat sandstone pieces, 0.20 m by 0.30 m, blackened on the top surface and fragmented; that of the smaller chamber was composed of tile, which was a re-flooring above a reddened surface below.

The flue was built in the thickness of the end wall of the hall, and was of bifid construction to serve both chambers. The roof tiles used in its construction were reddened and blackened. The floor of the flue was considerably lower than the floors of the chambers. One of these succeeded the other, and the flue position was not changed; but it was altered to its bifid form to accommodate the later chamber. The flue lies at the intersection of the two arcs of the chambers. The mouth of the flue was about 1.25 m wide, and the longer flue, serving the larger chamber, was 1.70 m in length. No carbonised grain was identified, but many ash layers existed within the building, containing burnt wood fragments; the ash had probably been raked out hot, thus burning the floor layers of the hall.

If these are interpreted as grain drying kilns, then the arrangement of flue and drying chamber can be paralleled in some nineteenth-century corn drying barns in the north of Scotland and the Shetlands, (Jamieson 1968; Scott 1951). The circular drying chamber adjoins the building, and is served by a fireplace within the thickness of the end wall of the barn, or just inside the barn. The flue is not horizontal, but rises up from the fireplace to the drying chamber, either with a gentle slope, or more or less vertically.

However, the heat generated would not be intense enough to produce the consistent burning noticed all over the floors of these two structures. Could these, therefore, be better explained as being large ovens? – having a fire burning inside them to raise the heat within, which was then raked out and the food placed inside; the heat being maintained by a fire in the flue. Unfortunately, not enough of the superstructure of these two kilns or ovens survived to prove or disprove this by the presence of arched or square openings in the end wall. These would have been for access into the ovens, and are characteristic of structures of this type.

Editor's note: These excavations have since been published (Stevens and Stevens 1991).

K42: Tintagel (Cornwall, England)

Coordinates: 205080, 89030

Source: Ralegh-Radford 1939

Illustration: Figure 42

Site type: Monastery

Date: 6th-9th century

On site D, 'in the angle of one room set against the rock is a circular flue which probably belonged to an oven. Such structures are known to have been used at this period for drying corn' (Ralegh-Radford 1939). It was not possible to visit this site, so little can be said to amplify this description. The plan of the building shows a platform in one corner with a circular opening in it. It may be that this is a drying chamber, but the absence of any reference to a horizontal flue connecting this to a fireplace outside the platform may indicate that this is an emplacement for a vat.

Editor's note: Much subsequent work has since been undertaken at Tintagel (see, for instance, Bowden and Jamieson 2016). Excavations undertaken in 2016-17 have suggested that some settlement remains previously dated to the 5th-6th centuries may in fact date from as late as the 10th century (Susan Greaney, pers. comm.; publication in prep. by Cornwall Archaeology Unit).

Figure 42 - Drying kiln at Tintagel (photograph by Sue Greaney).

K43: Merthyr Dyfan (Glamorgan, Wales)

Coordinates: 311345, 169485

Source: not specified

Site type: not specified

Date: Medieval

Circular or oval stone-lined pit dug into a stream bank, similar to Beere kilns (**K21**). Information was requested but no reply was received.

Insufficient Evidence for Type

This section contains kilns about which not enough is known to place them in any of the types above. This is partly a result of excavators not replying to enquiries about kilns; partly due to a lack of time to see or enquire about some kilns; and lastly because parts of the structure have been destroyed or were not excavated.

- **K44:** Alcester (Warwickshire, England)
- **K45:** Block Eary (Isle of Man)
- **K46:** Deddington Castle (Oxfordshire, England)
- **K47:** Inishkea North (Co. Mayo, Ireland)
- **K48:** Lincoln (Lincolnshire, England)
- **K49:** Northampton (Northamptonshire, England)
- **K50:** Rhuddlan (Denbighshire, Wales)
- **K51:** Scole (Norfolk, England)
- **K52:** Spaunton New Inn (North Yorkshire, England)
- **K53:** Sutton (Shropshire, England)
- **K54:** Thetford (Norfolk, England)
- **K55:** Wallingford Castle (Oxfordshire, England)

K44: Alcester (Warwickshire, England)

Coordinates: 408555, 257555

Source: Excavated 1968-9. The information below was kindly sent by Mr S. Taylor.

Site type: Town site

Date: Medieval

A free-standing kiln, built of local Arden Sandstone, was found. The stone had not undergone much heating. No evidence was found of the type of fuel used. It is not known what was dried in this kiln.

K45: Block Eary (Isle of Man)

Coordinates: 240055, 489575

Source: Gelling 1963

Site type: Shieling

Date: Norse to 13th or 14th century

A mound, later remodelled as an animal pen, may have been a corn drying kiln in its first phase. Below the paved floor of this pen there was a deposit of peat ash, 0.25 m deep, from wall to wall, with a layer of clean gravel interleaved in it.

On the lower side of the mound, facing down the valley, there were the remains of two short 'arms' of turf, 0.60 m apart, with a few associated stones. These may originally have been part of a flue, which led to a drying chamber in the centre of the mound.

These 'arms' or 'horns' can be seen as part of similar earthworks of disused corn drying kilns of post-medieval date in Scotland and the north of England. In each case they are flues. The Toe, Bewcastle, in Cumberland, is a good example (Ramm *et al.* 1972). But this does not prove the structure found at Block Eary to be a drying kiln.

K46: Deddington Castle (Oxfordshire, England)

Coordinates: 446555, 231555

Source: Jope and Threlfall 1958. Excavated by Professor E.M. Jope.

Site type: Castle

Date: Later medieval

A grain drying kiln was found in a barn. Further information was requested but was not received.

K47: Inishkea North (Co. Mayo, Ireland)

Coordinates: 57009, 322530

Source: Henry 1951

Site type: Farmstead

Date: After 7th century

'Immediately beside a granary was discovered a complicated arrangement of drying kiln with a flue covered by flagstones encrusted with soot. The great number of querns and fragments of querns found in every part of the house confirm the impression that some kind of grain – oats, barley or wheat – played an important part of the life of the people who lived in it' (Henry 1951).

Further information was requested but was not received.

K48: Lincoln (Lincolnshire, England)

Coordinates: 497600, 371960

Source: Excavated by Miss C. Colyer.

Site type: Town site

Date: Medieval

Several drying kilns have been excavated. It was not possible to see the records of these kilns, owing to lack of time.

Editor's note: These and other excavations have since been published (Steane 2002).

K49: Northampton (Northamptonshire, England)

Coordinates: 475555, 261555

Source: Selkirk and Selkirk 1974; excavated by Mr J. Williams (Williams 1974).

Site type: Town site

Date: 15th century

A pair of malt roasting ovens, well-built in stone, were found sunk into the ground (both resembling Type I).

Lack of time prevented further information being requested.

K50: Rhuddlan (Denbighshire, Wales)

Coordinates: 302555, 378555

Source: Selkirk and Selkirk 1972c; excavated by Mrs H. Miles.

Site type: Town site

Date: 11th century

A kiln, 3.05 m in diameter, had been used for drying fish and meat on a commercial scale.

Further information was requested but was not received.

Editor's note: Excavations at Rhuddlan have since been published (Quinnell *et al.* 1994).

K51: Scole (Norfolk, England)

Coordinates: 614355, 278955

Source: Hurst 1965; the information below was kindly by Miss B. Green.

Site type: Village

Date: 16th century or later

Part of this structure was discovered in a foundation trench for a bungalow, and it was impossible to expose it all. It consisted of a large area of burnt clay, at least 2.29 m by 1.83 m. It was perforated with small holes, with an average diameter of 0.05 m, scattered irregularly through it. A sixteenth-century sherd was embedded in this clay, and eleventh- to twelfth-century pottery was found in the surrounding area.

It was suggested that it may have been a corn drying kiln because the excavator could not think of anything else of that size. The evidence available suggests some other type of kiln, or drying shed, rather than a corn drying kiln. It may have been for the drying of bricks, tiles or pottery, for instance.

K52: Spaunton New Inn (North Yorkshire, England)

Coordinates: 472400, 489800

Source: Radley 1967; excavated by Mr R.H. Hayes.

Site type: Farmstead

Date: 12th 14th century

Beside a building of the 12th to 14th centuries was found a rock-cut possible drying kiln. It was 1.68 m long, 0.84 m wide, and 1.12 m deep.

Further information was requested but was not received.

Editor's note: Excavations at Spaunton have since been published (Hayes 1986).

K53: Sutton (Shropshire, England)

Coordinates: 350305, 310445

Source: Hurst 1969; excavated by W.E. Jenks.

Site type: Deserted medieval village

Date: Various dates, between the 12th and 17th centuries.

Seven ovens, one for corn drying, and another associated with a twin-staked shed, were found.

Attempts at getting the address of the excavator failed.

Editor's note: Excavations in this area have since been published (Barker *et al.* 1991).

K54: Thetford (Norfolk, England)

Coordinates: 587000, 283000

Source: Davison 1968

Site type: Town site

Date: Medieval

Corn drying kilns and thirteenth-century farm buildings were found overlying late Saxon deposits.

Lack of time prevented further information being obtained about these kilns.

Editor's note: Davison's excavations in Thetford have since been published (Dallas 1993).

K55: Wallingford Castle (Oxfordshire, England)

Coordinates: 460950, 189730

Source: Hurst 1967b; excavated by Mr N.P. Brooks.

Site type: Castle

Date: Possibly 12th century

Charred grains of wheat and rye were discovered from the ash deposits in two clay ovens of elongated form, one with a domed clay roof partially intact. This suggested that they were corn drying kilns.

Further information was requested but not received.

Editor's note: A major synthesis of the archaeology of Wallingford has since been published (Christie *et al.* 2013).

Not Drying Kilns

The following structures were published as possible drying kilns. The site records of the Winchester kiln, and the structure found in Elm Street, Stamford, were examined; the 'drying kiln' in the malthouse at Fountains Abbey was visited; and in my opinion these are not drying kilns, but structures of a different kind, and with different functions.

- **K56:** Fountains Abbey (North Yorkshire, England)
- **K57:** Stamford Elm Street (Lincolnshire, England)
- **K58:** Winchester (Hampshire, England)

K56: Fountains Abbey (North Yorkshire, England)

Coordinates: 427500, 468300

Source: Gilyard-Beer 1970

Illustration: Figures 43-45

Site type: Monastery malthouse

Date: Second half of the 13th century

In the guidebook, a circular stone structure, with a small flue on the east side, is described as 'a kiln for the final drying of malt under heat' (Gilyard-Beer 1970). This is 1.70 m in diameter at the top and 0.55 m deep. It has concave stone sides, burnt wine red for a considerable depth. The floor, also burnt consistently all over, has been worn in the middle by the repeated raking out of ashes.

A drying kiln would not require such intense heat as was obviously generated in this structure; and the burning is consistent all over and not just limited to the flue. The shape is perfect for holding a round vat (Figures 44-45); and the consistency and intensity of the heating could only have been produced by a vat in position, diverting the flames and heat to the sides of the structure. Thus, this structure would be better interpreted as a heated vat emplacement or boiler, with the fire burning directly below the vat; access to the fire is obtained through an arched opening on one side. This arrangement can be seen in an illustration of a medieval brewer (Figure 28).

One of two other internal structures in the south end of the malthouse may be a drying kiln. In the south-west corner there is a rectangular structure about 3.50 m east-west by 3.35 m north-south, with a narrow entrance in the north side, 1.37 m wide and 0.76 m long. To the east of this, in the middle of the south side and partly projecting outside it, is a large circular structure, 5.34 m in diameter. This has an entrance on its north side, about 1.40 m wide and about 0.50 m long. Either structure could be a drying kiln, the former one of Type II, and the latter one of Type V.

On the 1887-8 plan drawn by Brakspear (published in St John Hope 1900), the circular structure is labelled as a steeping vat. If the rectangular structure is then interpreted as a drying kiln, this juxtaposition of circular steeping vat and rectangular drying kiln can be paralleled at Grafton Regis in the brewhouse (**K8**). However, rectangular vats are not unknown, such as at Lindisfarne, in the monastery brewhouse (Ministry of Public Building and Works 1970).

This end of the malthouse at Fountains Abbey lies below a field. The existence of burning around the entrances of either of these structures may suggest which one was the drying kiln. However, owing to lack of time, it was not possible to obtain further information to solve this problem.

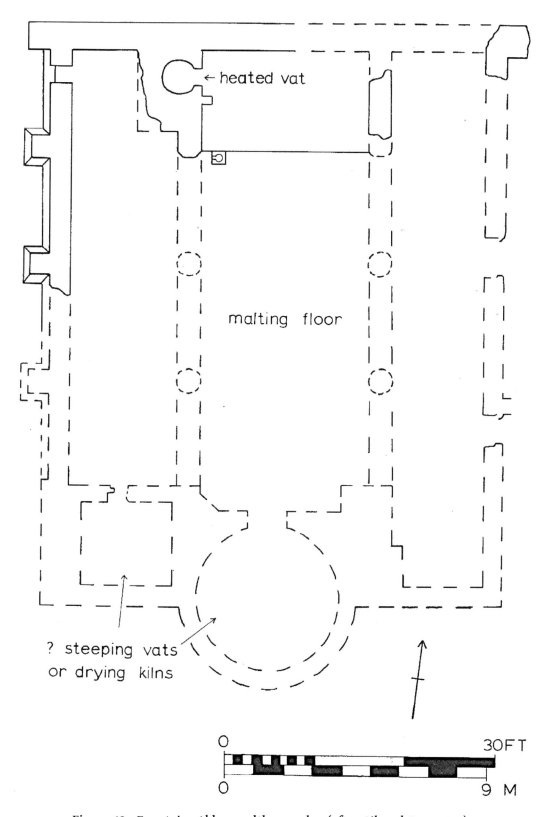

← heated vat

malting floor

? steeping vats
or drying kilns

0   30FT

0   9 M

Figure 43 - Fountains Abbey malthouse plan (after Gilyard-Beer 1970).

Figure 44 - Fountains Abbey malthouse: heated vat emplacement, from east. Photograph by R.J. Rickett.

Figure 45 - Fountains Abbey malthouse from south-east. Burning on floor shows original position of sides of flue. Scale 0.20 m. Photograph by R.J. Rickett.

K57: Stamford (Lincolnshire, England)

Coordinates: 503155, 307155

Source: Cherry 1972; the information below was kindly put at my disposal by Miss C.M. Mahany.

Illustration: Figure 46

Site type: Town site

Date: 13th century

Excavated in Elm Street, site O. A circular stone structure was discovered with a stokehole at the west end. Between these two, a double arched flue originally existed, from which two horizontal channels on either side of a central ridge led into the circular structure. After a period of use, the interior was re-lined and reduced, and rounded in shape.

The stones, clay and soil of which this structure was built had been consistently burnt bright red. This great heat would have been too great for drying anything placed above it. Originally interpreted as a drying kiln, this should probably be better interpreted as a large oven.

Similar parallel flues with such evidence of burning, found at King John's Hunting Lodge, Writtle (Rahtz 1969), have been interpreted as a possible bread oven or cooking range.

Figure 46 - Stamford Elm Street oven from south-west (C.M. Mahany). Scale 6 ft.

K58: Winchester (Hampshire, England)

Coordinates: 448355, 129555

Source: Moorhouse 1971; the excavator, Mr M. Biddle, kindly let me see the records of this kiln.

Illustration: Figure 47

Site type: Town site

Date: 15th to 16th century

On the Cathedral Green was found a 'double flued circular kiln, perhaps for malting, sealed by the latest masons' chippings, can perhaps be related to the *bracinum* or brewery, known to have been in the area in the 15th century' (Moorhouse 1971).

The sides of the kiln battered outwards, and the flues led into the base of it at either side. The whole of the interior had been burnt bright red to a considerable depth, and some of the stones had crumbled under this heat. On either side, behind the flues, large oblong areas sloped downwards to the kiln. The layers associated with these consisted of flint and chalk fragments, burnt mortar (lime remains?), and charcoal. The kiln was filled with masons' chippings, covering the bottom layers of mortar and charcoal.

The evidence suggests that this was a lime kiln to provide the Cathedral masons with lime for mortar. The oblong areas behind the flues would have been for the raking out of lime formed in the kiln; and the kiln would have been charged from above with layers of charcoal and chalk, or other calcareous rock.

A similar kiln at Ogmore Castle, Glamorgan, had a circular chamber with battered sides, with a flue at either side. This was identified as a lime kiln (Ralegh-Radford 1971).

Editor's note: See now Biddle and Rickett 1990.

Figure 47 - Medieval kiln excavated in Winchester, Cathedral Green, 1970. © Winchester Excavations Committee (not to be reproduced without written permission).

Appendix: The Brewhouse and Bakehouse at Grafton Regis, Northamptonshire

Robert Rickett (1976)

The medieval monastic food allowance permitted a gallon of good ale per day per person, often with a second gallon of weak ale (Salzman 1913). Many monasteries were provided with malthouses and brewhouses, which had malting kilns: such as at Fountains Abbey (**K56**); Kirkstall Abbey (**K29**), Nunkeeling Priory in the East Riding of Yorkshire (Gilyard-Beer 1958), Tynemouth Priory in Tyne and Wear (Hadcock 1952), and here at Grafton Regis. Monastic Granges, such as Aldborough in North Yorkshire, and Duleek in Co. Meath, also had such facilities (Platt 1969).

William Harrison, in his *Description of England*, originally published in 1587, has a full description of the malting and brewing process (Harrison 1587). Any cereal grain can be converted into malt by the germination of wheat, rye, or oats, or a mixture of different grains, but barley was considered to be the best (Salzman 1913; *Encyclopædia Britannica*: 'malt'). The discovery of grains of oats and barley in the Grafton Regis malt kiln is interesting; this combination is known as dredge or drage (Harvey 1965: 48). This was commonly used in brewing, as a diary of a country household testifies: 'Mon Oct 3 (1412): The Brewing: 2 quarters of malt, whereof 1 quarter drage, whence came 112 gallons of ale' (Rickert 1948: 87).

The grain was first put in a large lead cistern and steeped in water to make it swell, then it was spread on the malting floor to germinate. It was regularly raked, over several weeks, to ensure uniform growth. When it had germinated sufficiently, it was put on the kiln to dry, spread about 8 cm thick on a hair cloth over a wooden frame. The drying burnt off the shoots, arresting the growth of the barley, and converted it into malt. The process took from one to four days, depending on the type of malt required; and this also determined the heat of the fire. It was periodically turned during drying with malt shovels and forks. The malted grain was then ground and used to brew ale, for which coppers for boiling and vats for cooling and fermenting were needed (Brakspear 1905; Harrison 1587; Steer 1969).

Archaeology and documentary references show us the layout of malt- and brewhouses and the kind of equipment used in them. Steeping vat emplacements have been found at Grafton Regis and at Fountains Abbey (**K56**), where there is a malting floor with a drain. In the Grafton Regis brewhouse, the malt would either have been placed on the area in the centre of the building, or on the first floor. In the 19th and early 20th centuries, malthouses had three floors for the germination of grain (Evans 1970: 246, 260).

Inventories of monastic institutions made at the Dissolution list malting and brewing equipment such as steeping cisterns, malt kilns, brewing leads, mash vats, and wooden tubs or metal vats for cooling and fermenting. For example, the Inventory of the Late Priory of St Thomas Nyghe Stafford contains the following entry: 'The Brewhouse and Bakehouse – ij brewing leades; iJ fattes; vj wort leades; j panne in a furneshe; j steping sesterne; j here for the kill [haircloth for the malt kiln]', and from a similar building at Burton-on-Trent 'a presse and a trough' are mentioned (Walcott 1871: 211, 230). In the post-medieval period, brewhouse inventories became more comprehensive, and items such as malting forks and shovels, scoops, pails, bowls and vessels, ladles and taps are mentioned (Peacock 1884: 133, 148; Steer 1969).

The above mention of a pan in a furnace is repeated elsewhere, such as at Barnewell Priory, Cambridgeshire (Walcott 1871: 224), where it states that it is made of brass. These must be coppers or heated vats, the existence of which is implied from the evidence at Grafton Regis. The circular stone structures in the north-west and south-east corners of the building could either be ovens or heated vat emplacements. A 15th century illustration of a medieval brewer from *The Housekeeping Book of the Twelve Mendel Brothers* (Figure 28) shows a heated vat, sitting in a vertical-sided stone structure. A fire is burning below the vat and is obviously stoked from the arched opening in the side. However, one type of medieval baking oven is known to have been heated from below, also stoked through an arched opening (Rickert 1948). A heated vat emplacement can be seen in the brewhouse at Fountains Abbey (**K56**), which is actually shaped to take a round-bottomed vat; but at Grafton Regis the archaeological evidence is not conclusive either way.

Many references to kiln hairs or hair cloths occur in connection with malting kilns. The earliest known to me is from the 13th century: in 1278-9, one was purchased for the oven/kiln at Cuxham, Oxfordshire: 'in 1 heyre empt ad Braseum siccandum [to dry malt] 3s' (Harvey 1965: 38). These consisted of a finely woven cloth of horse hair, presumably stretched across a wooden frame (Barley in Corder 1961: 55; Steer 1969), or across hurdles (Harvey 1965: 38). A reference to the manufacture of kiln hairs occurs in the city records of York for 1487. Other types of movable drying floors are known, such as wooden joists on which straw was spread in tightly-packed bundles, and in the post-medieval period, a linen sheet was sometimes placed on top of the straw bedding (Scott 1951).

The grain on the floor of the Grafton Regis kiln must have got there by the accidental burning and collapse of the drying floor or kiln hair above, resulting in the burning of the grain upon it; or as a result of small particles slipping through it during the placing of the grain on the drying floor, or during its subsequent turning during drying. Various methods were used to prevent the drying floor or kiln hair catching alight from the fire in the flue. In medieval kilns of this type, evidence of two different methods has been found. A kiln with an arched flue between stokehole and drying chamber was found at Montgomery Castle (**K5**). In the kiln found at 36 High Street, Stamford (**K6**), a baffle stone was found *in situ*, placed at the same angle as the battered side of the drying chamber through which the flue entered.

The type of fuel used in these kilns must have depended upon what was available in the locality; various fuels were therefore used in kilns around the country – wood and charcoal, furze, brushwood, peat, turf, and straw, the latter probably bound by withies into faggots. Straw was considered to be the best fuel for malting, but fern or wood were also used. For malting, the type of fuel often added additional flavours to the drink.

The Grafton Regis drying kiln is similar in form to others at Brixworth (**K9**), Faxton (**K10**) and Barrow (**K7**). These all have square or rectangular drying chambers with partly walled stokeholes. Only the Barrow kiln is known to be contained within a building. Other very similar kilns, with completely enclosed stokeholes, and in the majority of cases with steps in the side for access, have been found at Great Casterton (**K4**), Montgomery Castle (**K5**), 36 High Street, Stamford (**K6**), two in buildings in Stamford Castle Bailey (**K2, K3**), and at Northampton (**K49**).

These two types of drying kiln occur predominantly in south-west Lincolnshire, Rutland and Northamptonshire. They make their first appearance in the 13th century, and the basic form has remained unchanged up to recent times, in this area and elsewhere in the country.

The use of the Grafton Regis drying kiln need not have been restricted to malting; food grain and other crops may have been dried periodically as the need arose. The kiln would most probably have been used to harden grain before grinding, making it easier to break the outer layer (Curwen 1938: 151).

Similarly, the large oven adjoining the west end of the bake- and brewhouse at Grafton Regis could have been multi-purpose. Such ovens were pre-heated by burning faggots inside them, the ashes of which were raked out when it had reached the required temperature; then bread or other food was placed inside and the entrance sealed. The use of identical ovens in the post-medieval period is well documented (Evans 1965: 55–59).

The Dissolution inventories also show the kind of equipment used for making bread, as well as for brewing. That of Burton-on-Trent is a typical example: 'The Bruehouse and Bakehouse – ij furnes of ledd, xiij wort ledds ian iij frames, j grett malt fatte, j yelyng ffatte, a cesterne of ledd, a presse and a trough, a table bord, a bultyng whych, ij tridds and ij trourghes, a moldyng table' (Walcott 1871).

Baking and brewing were often combined in the same building, for several reasons. As ale and bread were an important part of the medieval diet, one monk was in charge of both, sometimes living in the bake- and brewhouse, such as at Fountains Abbey (**K56**). Common ingredients such as grain and yeast, and common equipment, made it more convenient. Both processes require warmth and in this respect they would complement each other.

Editor's note: Excavations at Grafton Regis (**K8**) were undertaken in the 1960s, led by the late Christine Mahany and funded by the Department for the Environment. This report was written in relation to these excavations, which at the time of writing remain unpublished. Mr Rickett's report is published here by kind permission of Historic England, successor to the Department for the Environment for these purposes.

Bibliography

Encyclopædia Britannia, 14th edition. 1970. Chicago: Encyclopædia Britannica Inc.

Addyman, P. V. 1963. Note on a kiln-like structure at Buckden, Hunts. *Medieval Archaeology* 6–7: 12–14.

Alcock, L. 1972. "By South Cadbury is that Camelot ...": the excavation of Cadbury Castle. London: Thames Hudson.

Allen, M., Lodwick, L., Brindle, T., Fulford, M. and Smith, A. 2017. *New Visions of the Countryside of Roman Britain Volume 2: The Rural Economy of Roman Britain.* London: Society for the Promotion of Roman Studies.

Baddelay, W.S.C. 1910. The manor and site of Hullasey. *Transactions of the Bristol and Gloucestershire Archaeological Society* 33: 338–354.

Barker, P., Haldon, R. and Jenks, W. 1991. Excavations on Sharpstones hill near Shrewsbury, 1965-71. *Transactions of the Shropshire Archaeological and Historical Society* 67: 15–57.

Barley, M.W. 1961. *The English farmhouse and cottage.* London: Routledge and Kegan Paul.

Bennett, H.S. 1960. Life on the English manor: a study of peasant conditions, 1150-1400. Cambridge: Cambridge University Press.

Beresford, G. 1979. Three deserted medieval settlements on Dartmoor: a report on the late E. Marie Minter's excavations. *Medieval Archaeology* 23: 98–158.

Biddle, M. and Rickett, R. 1990. A possible limekiln, in M. Biddle, *Object and Economy in Medieval Winchester*: 318-320. Oxford: Clarendon Press.

Bolton, E.G. 1960. Excavations of a house and malt kiln at Barrow, Rutland. *Medieval Archaeology* 4: 128–131.

Bowden, M. and Jamieson, E. 2016. *Tintagel Castle and Island, Cornwall: archaeological survey enhancement.* Swindon: English Heritage Research Department.

Brakspear, H. 1905. *Waverley Abbey.* London: Surrey Archaeological Society.

Britnell, W. 1984. A 15th-century corn drying kiln from Collfryn, Llansantffraid Deuddwr, Powys. *Medieval Archaeology* 28: 190–194.

Brunskill, R.W. 1970. *Illustrated handbook of vernacular architecture.* London: Faber and Faber.

Butler, L. 1987. Domestic buildings in Wales and the evidence of the Welsh Laws. *Medieval Archaeology* 32: 47–58.

Butler, L. and Gerrard, C. 2021. Faxton: Excavations in a deserted Northamptonshire village 1966-68. London: Routledge.

Carus-Wilson, E. 1963. The medieval trade of the ports of the Wash. *Medieval Archaeology* 6–7: 182–201.

Carver, M. 2010. The Birth of a Borough. An Archaeological Study of Anglo-Saxon Stafford. Woodbridge: Boydell Press.

Cherry, J. 1972. Medieval Britain in 1971. Part II. *Medieval Archaeology* 16: 171–212.

Cherry, J. 1973. Medieval Britain in 1972. Part II. *Medieval Archaeology* 17: 153–188.

Christie, N., Creighton, O., Edgeworth, M., Hamerow, H. and Archibald, M. 2013. *Transforming townscapes: from burh to borough: the archaeology of Wallingford, AD 800-1400.* London: Society for Medieval Archaeology.

Cocks, A. 1921. A Romano-British homestead in the Hambleden Valley, Buckinghamshire. *Archaeologia* 81: 141–198.

Collis, J.R. 1968. Excavations at Owlesbury, Hants. *Antiquaries Journal* 48: 18–31.

Comeau, R. and Burrow, S. 2021. Grain dryers in Wales from the late Iron Age to the Sixteenth Century: a Gazetteer. *Archaeologia Cambrensis* 170.

Corder, P. 1954. The Roman Town and Villa at Great Casterton, Rutland: Second Report for the years 1951-1953. Nottingham: University of Nottingham.

Corder, P. 1961. The Roman Town and Villa at Great Casterton, Rutland: Third Report for the years 1954-1958. Nottingham: University of Nottingham.

Coulton, G.G. 1925. *The Medieval Village.* Cambridge: Cambridge University Press.

Cracknell, S. and Mahany, C. 1994. Roman Alcester: Southern Extramural Area. 1964-1966 Excavations. Part 2: Finds and Discussion. York: Council for British Archaeology.

Cubbon, A.M. and Megaw, B.R.S. 1969. Corn drying kilns in the Isle of Man. *Journal of the Manx Museum* 7(85): 113–117.

Curwen, E.C. 1933. Excavations on Thundersbarrow Hill, Sussex. *Antiquaries Journal* 13: 109–151.

Curwen, E.C. 1938. Early Agriculture in Denmark. *Antiquity* 12(46): 135–153.

Dallas, C. 1993. Excavations in Thetford by B.K. Davison between 1964 and 1970. Gressenhall: Norfolk Museums Service.

Davey, P. 2014. *The Isle of Man in Medieval Times.* Stroud: Amberley.

Davies, O. 1938. Kilns for flax drying and lime burning. *Ulster Journal of Archaeology* 1.

Davison, B.K. 1968. The late Saxon town of Thetford; an interim report on the 1964-66 excavations. *Medieval Archaeology* 11: 189–209.

Dixon, P. 2011. Of bannocks and ale: cereal processing in Scotland, c.1100-1750, in J. Klápště and P. Sommer (eds) *Processing, Storage, Distribution of Food. Food in the Medieval Rural Environment* (Ruralia VIII): 155-172. Turnhout: Brepols.

Dundas, J. 1866. Notes on the excavation of an ancient building at Tapock, in the Torwood, Parish of Dunipace, count of Stirling. *Proceedings of the Society of Antiquaries of Scotland* 6: 259–265.

Evans, E.E. 1945. *Irish heritage: the landscape, the people and their work.* Dundalk: W. Tempest, Dundalgan Press.

Evans, E.E. 1957. *Irish folk ways.* London: Routledge and Kegan Paul.

Evans, G.E. 1965. *Ask the fellows who cut the hay.* London: Faber and Faber.

Evans, G.E. 1970. Where beards wag all: the relevance of the oral tradition. London: Faber and Faber.

Fairhurst, H. 1969. The Deserted Settlement at Lix, West Perthshire. *Proceedings of the Society of Antiquaries of Scotland* 101: 160–199.

Faulkner, N. and Blakelock, E. 2020. The excavation of a Mid Anglo-Saxon malthouse at Sedgeford, Norfolk: an interim report. *Anglo-Saxon Studies in Archaeology and History* 22: 68–95.

Feachem, R.W. 1957. Castlehill Wood Dun, Stirlingshire. *Proceedings of the Society of Antiquaries of Scotland* 90: 24–51.

Fenton, A. 1963. Grain Drying Kilns in Shetland. *Shetland News* 25.9.63.

Fenton, A. 1978. *The Northern Isles: Orkney and Shetland*. Edinburgh: John Donald.

Forbes, R. 1954. Food and drink, in C. Singer, E. Holmyard, A. Hall and T. Williams (eds) *A History of Technology Volume II*: 103-146. Oxford: Clarendon Press.

Funnell, J. 2009. A medieval moated site at Stretham, near Henfield, West Sussex. *Sussex Archaeological Collections* 147: 77–95.

Gelling, P.S. 1963. Medieval shielings in the Isle of Man. *Medieval Archaeology* 6–7: 156–172.

Gelling, P.S. 1970. A Norse homestead near Doarlish Cashen, Kirkpatrick, Isle of Man. *Medieval Archaeology* 14: 74–82.

Gilyard-Beer, R. 1951. *The Romano-British baths at Well*. Leeds: Yorkshire Archaeological Society.

Gilyard-Beer, R. 1958. Abbeys: an introduction to the religious houses of England and Wales. London: H.M. Stationery Office.

Gilyard-Beer, R. 1970. *Fountains Abbey, North Yorkshire*. London: H.M. Stationery Office.

Glanville Jones, G.R. 1960. The pattern of settlement on the Welsh Border. *Agricultural History Review* 8: 66–81.

Goodchild, R.G. 1943. T-shaped Corn-drying Ovens in Roman Britain. *The Antiquaries Journal* 23: 148–153.

Hadcock, R.N. 1952. *Tynemouth Priory and Castle, Northumberland*. London: H.M. Stationery Office.

Hamerow, H. 2012. *Rural Settlements and Society in Anglo-Saxon England*. Oxford: Oxford University Press.

Hamilton-Thompson, A. 1949. *Lindisfarne Priory, Northumberland*. London: H.M. Stationery Office.

Hamilton, J.R.C. 1956. *Excavations at Jarlshof*. London: H.M. Stationery Office.

Hardy, A., Charles, B.M. and Williams, R.J. 2007. Death and taxes: the archaeology of a Middle Saxon estate centre at Higham Ferrers, Northamptonshire. Oxford: Oxford Archaeology.

Harrison, W. 1587. *The Description of England* (G. Edelen, ed. 1968). Ithaca, NY: Cornell University Press.

Harvey, P. 1965. A medieval Oxfordshire village: Cuxham, 1240 to 1400. London: Oxford University Press.

Hayes, R. 1986. Excavations at Spaunton Manor, N Yorkshire. *Ryedale Historian* 13: 4–25.

Heaton, M.J. 1993. Two Mid-Saxon Grain-driers and Later Medieval Features at Chantry Fields, Gillingham, Dorset. *Proceedings of the Dorset Natural History and Archaeology Society* 114: 97–126.

Henry, F. 1951. Habitation sites from Inishkea North, Co. Mayo. *Journal of the Royal Society of Antiquaries of Ireland* 81: 75–76.

Hijmans, R. and University of California, Berkeley, Museum of Vertebrate Zoology, 2015, Boundary, Isle of Man, 2015. UC Berkeley, Museum of Vertebrate Zoology, viewed 29 June 2021, <http://purl.stanford.edu/nk743nh6214>.

Hildyard, E.J.W. and Snowdon, G.V. 1955. Allerton Wood, in *Archaeology of Weardale: sixth summary of research, 1950-52*: 15-16. Stanhope: E.J.W. Hildyard.

Hinton, D. and Peacock, D. 2020. Impinging on the Past: A Rescue Excavation at Fladbury, Worcestershire, 1967. Southampton: Highfield Press.

His Majesty's Stationery Office. 1910. Calendar of the Patent Rolls preserved in the Public Record Office. Henry III. AD 1258-1266. Volume V. London: H.M. Stationery Office.

Horsburgh, J. 1868. Notes of Cromlechs, duns, hut circles, chambered cairns and remains, in the county of Sutherland. *Proceedings of the Society of Antiquaries of Scotland* 7: 273.

Hoskins, W.G. 1965. The Midland Peasant: the economic and social history of a Leicestershire village. London: Macmillan.

Hughes, K. 1972. Early Christian Ireland, an Introduction to the Sources. London: Hodder and Stoughton.

Hurst, D.G. 1963. Medieval Britain in 1961. Part II. *Medieval Archaeology* 6–7: 313–349.

Hurst, D.G. 1964. Medieval Britain in 1962-3. Part II. *Medieval Archaeology* 8: 241–299.

Hurst, D.G. 1965. Medieval Britain in 1964. Part II. *Medieval Archaeology* 9: 178–220.

Hurst, D.G. 1966. Medieval Britain in 1965. Part II. *Medieval Archaeology* 10: 177–219.

Hurst, D.G. 1967a. Post-medieval Britain in 1966. *Post-Medieval Archaeology* 1: 107–121.

Hurst, D.G. 1967b. Medieval Britain in 1966. Part II. *Medieval Archaeology* 11: 272–319.

Hurst, D.G. 1969. Medieval Britain in 1968. Part II. *Medieval Archaeology* 13: 243–287.

Hurst, D.G. 1970. Medieval Britain in 1969. Part II. *Medieval Archaeology* 14: 166–208.

Hurst, J.G. and Beresford, M.W. 1971. *Deserted Medieval Villages*. London: Lutterworth Press.

Jackson, G. 1956. The Story of Bolton Castle: an introduction to the Wensleydale fortress of the Scropes. Clapham: Dalesman Books.

Jamieson, E. 1968. The last of the corn kilns. *Scotlands Magazine* 64(3): 19–20.

Jope, E.M. and Ivens, R.J. 1998. The Rath at Ballymacash. *Proceedings of the Royal Irish Academy* 98(3): 101–123.

Jope, E.M. and Threlfall, R.I. 1958. Excavations of a medieval settlement at Beere, North Tawton, Devon. *Medieval Archaeology* 2: 112–140.

Joyce, P.W. 1903. *A Social History of Ancient Ireland, II*. London: Longmans, Green and Co.

Knight, J. 1992. Excavations at Montgomery Castle Part I: the documentary evidence, structures and excavated features. *Archaeologia Cambrensis* 141: 97–180.

Knox, H.T. 1907. Notes on gig mills and drying kilns near Ballyhaunis, Co. Mayo. *Proceedings of the Royal Irish Academy* 26c: 265–274.

Kuhn, S.M. and Reidy, J. (eds) 1969. *Middle English Dictionary*. Ann Arbor: University of Michegan Press.

Loyn, H.R. 1962. Anglo-Saxon England and the Norman Conquest. London: Longmans.

Macalister, R.A.S. and Praeger, R.L. 1928. Report on excavations of Uisneach. *Proceedings of the Royal Irish Academy* 38c: 69–127.

MacCormick, A. 2001. Nottingham's underground maltings and other medieval caves. *Transactions of the Thoroton Society of Nottinghamshire* 105: 73–99.

Mahany, C. 1977. Excavations at Stamford Castle Lincolnshire 1971-6. *Château Gaillard* 8: 223–245.

Mahany, C. 1994. Roman Alcester: Southern Extramural Area. 1964-1966 Excavations. Part 1: Stratigraphy and Structures. York: Council for British Archaeology.

Mahany, C., Burchard, A. and Simpson, G. 1982. *Excavations in Stamford, Lincolnshire, 1963-69.* London: Society for Medieval Archaeology.

Marshall, D. and Taylor, I. 1977. The excavation of the chambered cairn at Glenvoidean, Isle of Bute. *Proceedings of the Society of Antiquaries of Scotland* 108: 1–39.

Marshall, D.N. 1969. The story of the excavation of the neolithic burial cairn at Glenvoidean. *Transactions of the Bute Natural History Society* 17: 39–44.

Mayes, P. 1964. Sandal Castle: a short account of the history of the site and the 1964 excavations. Wakefield: Wakefield Historical Society.

Mayes, P., Butler, L. and Johnson, S. 1983. *Sandal Castle excavations, 1964-1973: a detailed archaeological report.* Wakefield: Wakefield Historical Publications.

McDonald, R. 2019. The sea kings: the Late Norse kingdoms of Man and the Isles c.1066-1275. Edinburgh: John Donald.

McKerracher, M. 2014a. Agricultural Development in Mid Saxon England. Unpublished DPhil dissertation, University of Oxford.

McKerracher, M. 2014b. Landscapes of Production in Mid Saxon England: the monumental grain ovens. *Medieval Settlement Research* 29: 82–85.

McKerracher, M. 2018. Farming Transformed in Anglo-Saxon England: Agriculture in the Long Eighth Century. Oxford: Windgather.

Mercer, J. 1972. Roomed and roomless grain drying kilns: the Hebridean boundary? *Ancient Monuments Society Transactions* 19: 27–36.

Milligan, I.D. 1963. Corn kilns in Bute. *Transactions of the Bute Natural History Society* 15: 53–59.

Ministry of Public Building and Works. 1970. *Lindisfarne Priory, Northumberland.* London: H.M. Stationery Office.

Monk, M. and Power, O. 2012. More than a grain of truth from a rash of corn-drying kilns? *Archaeology Ireland* 26(100): 38–41.

Monk, M. and Power, O. 2014. Casting light from the fires of corn-drying kilns on the Later Irish Iron Age. *Archaeology Ireland* 28(3): 38–42.

Monk, M. 1981. Post-Roman Drying Kilns and the Problem of Function: a preliminary statement, in D. Ó Corráin (ed.) *Irish Antiquity. Essays and Studies presented to Professor M.J. O'Kelly*: 216-230. Cork: Tower Books.

Monk, M. and Kelleher, E. 2005. An Assessment of the Archaeological Evidence for Irish Corn-Drying Kilns in the Light of the Results of Archaeological Experiments and Archaeobotanical Studies. *The Journal of Irish Archaeology* 14: 77–114.

Moore, B.F.E. 1958. Altmush corn drying kiln. *Meath Archaeological and Historical Society* 1(4): 75.

Moorhouse, S.A. 1971. Medieval Britain in 1970, Part II. *Medieval Archaeology* 15: 137–179.

Morris, P. 1979. *Agricultural Buildings in Roman Britain*. Oxford: British Archaeological Reports.

Murray, J.A.H. 1888. *New English Dictionary of Historical Principles*. Oxford: Clarendon Press.

Norris, N.E.S. and Burstow, G.P. 1950. A prehistoric and Romano-British site at West Blatchington, Hove. *Sussex Archaeological Collections* 89: 1–56.

O'Sullivan, A., McCormick, F., Kerr, T. and Harney, L. 2014. *Early Medieval Ireland, AD 400-1100. The Evidence from Archaeological Excavations*. Dublin: Royal Irish Academy.

Ó Ríordáin, S.P. 1942. The excavation of a large earthen ring fort at Garranes, Co. Cork. *Proceedings of the Royal Irish Academy* 47c: 77–150.

Ó Ríordáin, S.P. and Foy, J.B. 1941. Structure in Emlagh Townland. *Journal of the Cork Historical and Archaeological Society* 46: 98–99.

Ó Ríordáin, S.P. and Hartnett, P.S. 1944. The excavation of Ballycatteen fort, Co. Cork. *Proceedings of the Royal Irish Academy* 49c: 1–44.

Ó Ríordáin, S.P. and Macdermott, M.M. 1952. The excavation of a ring fort at Letterkeen, Co. Mayo. *Proceedings of the Royal Irish Academy* 54c: 89–119.

Parker, G. 1982. The Medieval Hermitage of Grafton Regis. *Northamptonshire Past and Present* VI(5): 247–252.

Peacock, E. 1884. Inventories made for Sir William and Sir Thomas Fairfax, knights of Walton, and of Gilling Castle, Yorks, in the 16th and 17th centuries. *Archaeologia* XLVIII: 121–156.

Pirie, E.J.E. 1966. *Kirkstall Abbey excavations, 1960-1964*. Leeds: Thoresby Society.

Pitt-Rivers, A.H.L.F. 1887. Excavations in Cranborne Chase, near Rushmore, on the borders of Dorset and Wilts. Volume I. London: Harrison and Sons.

Platt, C. 1969. The monastic grange in medieval England: a reassessment. London: Macmillan.

Proudfoot, V.B. 1961. The Economy of the Irish Rath. *Medieval Archaeology* 5(1): 94–122.

Quinnell, H., Blockley, M. and Berridge, P. 1994. *Excavations at Rhuddlan, Clwd: 1969-73 Mesolithic to Medieval.* York: Council for British Archaeology.

Radley, J. 1967. Yorkshire archaeological register. *Yorkshire Archaeological Journal* 42: 1–9.

Rahtz, P. 1969. Excavations at King John's Hunting Lodge, Writtle, Essex. 1955-57. London: Society for Medieval Archaeology.

Ralegh-Radford, C.A. 1939. *Tintagel Castle, Cornwall.* London: H.M. Stationery Office.

Ralegh-Radford, C.A. 1971. *Ogmore Castle, Glamorgan.* London: H.M. Stationery Office.

Ramm, H.G., McDowall, R.W. and Mercer, E. 1972. *Shielings and Bastles.* London: H.M. Stationery Office.

Reynolds, P.J. and Langley, J.K. 1979. Romano-British Corn-Drying Oven: An Experiment. *The Archaeological Journal* 136: 27–42.

Richards, M. 1954. *The Laws of Hywel Dda.* Liverpool: The University Press.

Rickert, E. 1948. *Chaucer's World.* London: Oxford University Press.

Rogers, A. (ed.) 1965. *The Making of Stamford.* Leicester: Leicester University Press.

Royal Commission on the Ancient and Historical Monuments of Scotland. 1971. *Argyll: An Inventory of the Ancient Monuments. Vol. I - Kintyre.* Glasgow: H.M. Stationery Office.

Salzman, L.F. 1913. English industries of the Middle Ages: being an introduction to the industrial history of medieval England. London: Constable.

Salzman, L.F. 1926. *English Life in the Middle Ages.* London: Oxford University Press.

Scott-Elliot, J. 1961. A corn drying kiln at Rue Farm, Dumfriesshire. *Transactions of the Dumfries and Galloway Historical and Antiquarian Society* 39: 80–82.

Scott, L. 1948. Note on Food Preservation. *Proceedings of the Prehistoric Society* 4: 124–125.

Scott, L. 1951. Corn-drying Kilns. *Antiquity* 25: 196–208.

Selkirk, A. and Selkirk, W. 1968a. Hereford. *Current Archaeology* 1: 242–246.

Selkirk, A. and Selkirk, W. 1968b. South Witham. *Current Archaeology* 1: 232–237.

Selkirk, A. and Selkirk, W. 1972a. Doncaster. *Current Archaeology* 3: 272–277.

Selkirk, A. and Selkirk, W. 1972b. Glenvoidean. *Current Archaeology* 3: 300.

Selkirk, A. and Selkirk, W. 1972c. Rhuddlan. *Current Archaeology* 3: 245–248.

Selkirk, A. and Selkirk, W. 1974. Northampton. *Current Archaeology* 4: 340–348.

Small, A. 1966. Excavations at Underhoull, Unst, Shetland. *Proceedings of the Society of Antiquaries of Scotland* 98: 225–248.

St John Hope, W. 1900. Fountains Abbey. *Yorkshire Archaeological Journal* 15: 269–402.

Steane, K. 2002. *The archaeology of the upper city and adjacent suburbs* (Lincoln Archaeological Studies 3). Oxford: Oxbow Books.

Steer, F.W. 1969. Farm and Cottage Inventories of mid-Essex, 1635-1749. London: Phillimore.

Stevens, L. and Stevens, P. 1991. Excavations on the South Lawn, Michelham Priory, Sussex, 1971-1976. *Sussex Archaeological Collections* 129: 45–80.

Thomas, H.J. 1967. Recent archaeological excavation and discovery in Glamorgan, Part III, Medieval period. *Morgannwg* 2: 82–83.

Trent and Peak Archaeology. 2015. The origins of Nottingham: archaeological investigations in the Medieval town from 1969 to 1980 [data-set]. York: Archaeological Data Service [distributor]. DOI: https://doi.org/10.5284/1029430.

van der Veen, M. 1989. Charred Grain Assemblages from Roman-Period Corn Driers in Britain. *The Archaeological Journal* 146: 302–319.

Walcott, M.E.C. 1871. Inventories and valuations of religious houses at the time of the Dissolution, from the Public Record Office. *Archaeologia* 43: 201–249.

Ward, J. 1907. Roman remains at Cwm-brwyn, Carmarthenshire. *Archaeologia Cambrensis* 7: 175–212.

Warhurst, C. 1969. Excavations at Rathbeg, Co. Antrim. *Ulster Journal of Archaeology* 32: 93–100.

Whitaker, I.R. 1957. Two Hebridean corn kilns. *Gwerin* 1: 161–170.

Whitney, W.D. (ed.) 1899. *The Century Dictionary*. New York: The Century Co.

Wild, J.P. 1973. *Durobrivae, A Review of Nene Valley Archaeology, I.* Peterborough: Nene Valley Research Committee.

Williams, J.H. 1974. Northampton: Saxon Concrete Mixer. *The Times*.

Wilson, D.R. 1961. Roman Britain in 1960, I – sites explored. *Journal of Roman Studies* 51: 155–191.

Wilson, D.R. 1966. Roman Britain in 1965, I – sites explored. *Journal of Roman Studies* 56: 196–217.

Wright, J. 1923. *English Dialect Dictionary*. London: Henry Frowde.

Young, C. 1972. The Oxford potteries. *Current Archaeology* 3: 209–211.